Calculations for the Leisure, Travel and Tourism Industries

Gordon E Gee

Formerly Head of Department of Food and Fashion,
South Downs College of Further Education
Havant, Hants

Formerly Examiner in Book-keeping and Food Costing
for the East Midlands Educational Union

Hodder & Stoughton

LONDON SYDNEY AUCKLAND TORONTO

Acknowledgments

Grateful acknowledgment is due to the following persons and organisations who have provided help and information in the writing of this book.

Avis Rent A Car Limited; British Airways; British Railways; Sarah Harison – Lecturer in Tourism, Eastleigh College; Gill Heighington – Lecturer in Tourism, Eastleigh College; Lewis Milkins, Wingsover Travel, Emsworth, Hampshire; Stephan Olszowski, Chairman and Marketing Director, Meon Travel Limited; P & O European Ferries; Yugotours Limited.

British Library Cataloguing in Publication Data
Gee, Gordon
    Calculations for leisure, travel and tourism.
    – (Calculations for industry)
    I. Title II. Series
    650.01

    ISBN 0–340–55152–6

First published 1991

© 1991 G E Gee

Typeset by Wearside Tradespools, Sunderland.
Printed in Great Britain for Hodder and Stoughton Educational and Academic, a division of Hodder and Stoughton Ltd, Mill Road, Dunton Green, Sevenoaks, Kent by Biddles Ltd.

Contents

— 1 —
Addition

Whatever job you have in the Travel, Tourism or Leisure Industries – if you are handling money, calculating bills, measuring, ordering goods or even checking your own wages, you should have the ability to add accurately and quickly. You may prefer to use a calculator but accuracy is still important and errors are sometimes made particularly with the position of decimal points.

Add the following:

1	547	2	2408	3	42	4	4908
	27		576		444		2385
	145		25		725		873

5	6754	6	1120	7	421	8	4402
	29		179		8532		3569
	3858		3558		5227		1197

9	hrs	mins	10	hrs	mins	11	hrs	mins	12	hrs	mins
	4	20		14	25		12	26		2	55
	3	18		3	40		1	50		10	40
	2	34		0	39		4	44		18	50

When adding British and foreign money, weights, liquids and lengths, decimals are sometimes used. Remember the first place behind the decimal point is the tenths column, the second place is the hundredths column, the third place is the thousandths etc. For example:

18.295 is 18 whole numbers, 2 tenths, 9 hundredths and 5 thousandths. Therefore 1 penny (one hundredth of a pound) can be written as £0.01 and 1 gram (g) can be written as 0.001 kg (because 1000 grams = 1 kilogram), 1 millilitre (ml) can be written as 0.001 litre (because 1000 ml = 1 litre) and 1 millimetre (mm) can be written as 0.001 metre (because 1000 mm = 1 metre)

> 7 kg 345 g can be written as 7.345 kg
> 15 litres 200 ml can be written as 15.200 litres or 15.2 litres
> 5 metres 25 mm can be written as 5.025 m

Some travel documents require height and weight expressed in metric amounts.

13 Write the following height in metres: 1 m 805 mm

14 Write the following weight in kg: 51 kg 640 g

A shipping company needs to know the length of all vehicles it transports.

15 A car had a length of 4 m 425 mm, write the length in metres.

16 The capacity of a water carrier is 8 litres 255 ml, express this amount in litres.

Add the following:

17		**18**		**19**		**20**	
	2.56		18.77		75.2		178.14
	18.14		64.08		208.425		464.3
	25.22		125.51		149.319		50.88

21	£	**22**	Francs	**23**	$	**24**	£
	47.32		125.05		0.25		0.05
	0.85		209.49		79.84		0.76
	22.48		4.56		0.76		0.95
	16.20		23.00		125.37		0.38

25	kg	**26**	kg	**27**	litres	**28**	metres
	7.255		21.39		145.672		2.155
	3.450		12.25		70.355		15.674
	11.268		148.94		14.845		25.305

Sometimes it is necessary to add horizontal columns of figures. Be careful to keep the tenths, hundredths and thousandths in the correct column.

Try your accuracy:

29 3.23 + 14.82 + 5.74

30 75.04 + 12.6 + 18.295

31 8.587 + 425.6 + 28 + 3.255

32 £14.07 + £0.09 + £2.82

33 £204.76 + £350.08 + £30 + £17.29

34 £7 + £89.40 + £329.88 + £120.07

35 £250.65 + £85 + £0.70 + £78.59

36 £3.27 + £0.49 + £38 + £408.66

37 5.675 m + 4.225 m + 13.480 m

38 19.255 kg + 205.675 kg + 64.050 kg.

— 2 —

Subtraction

Every day tens of thousands of subtraction calculations are performed by counter staff, cashiers and customers when purchases are made and change is required. On many occasions machines carry out the calculations but a customer would be wise to check.

1	748−	2	1395−	3	1105−	4	3252−
	345		288		197		2849

5	£	6	£	7	£	8	£
	34.29−		104.28−		300.00−		2460.45−
	5.74		97.39		127.18		895.63

9	Francs	10	$	11	£	12	£
	10.00−		5.00−		100.00−		1240.07−
	1.38		0.42		23.49		854.19

13	kg	14	kg	15	litres	16	metres
	17.239−		5.200−		15.270−		3.500−
	8.417		1.275		4.365		1.750

17	hrs mins	18	hrs mins	19	hrs mins	20	hrs mins
	10.30−		14.25−		10.08−		19.12−
	2.25		3.50		1.30		5.42

21 Write the answers to number 14 in grams.

22 Write the answer to number 15 in millilitres.

23 Write the answer to number 16 in millimetres.

24 £24.38 − £3.49   **25** £104.16   £98.36

26 £4.67 − £2.98   **27** £135.00 − £41.35

28 15.275 m − 5.280 m   **29** 150 kg − 55.125 kg

30 Find the difference between £441.85 and £376.47

31 By how much is £108.48 greater than £70.57?

32 By how much should 10.257 kg be increased to make 12 kg?

33 By how much is 3.28 m shorter than 7.275 m?

— 3 —

Multiplication

How good are you at tables?

1	6×5	**2**	4×7	**3**	3×12	**4**	9×6
5	7×7	**6**	8×3	**7**	4×12	**8**	11×11
9	6×7	**10**	9×9	**11**	4×5	**12**	6×3
13	12×12	**14**	9×8	**15**	8×7	**16**	12×11

Using tables:

17	124×5	**18**	423×7	**19**	302×9
20	213×25	**21**	357×63	**22**	841×123

When multiplying decimals, first work out the sum ignoring the decimal place, e.g.

$$5.64\times$$
$$\underline{7}$$
$$\overline{3948}$$

Next, count the number of figures behind the decimal point in the question and place the point so that there are the same number of figures behind the point in the answer.

$$5.64\times$$
$$\underline{7}$$
$$\overline{39.48}$$

Here is another example:

$$5.64\times$$
$$\underline{0.7}$$
$$\overline{3.948}$$

NB. The total number of figures behind the decimal point in the question was three (6, 4, 7). Notice how the answer is smaller than 5.64 when the number is multiplied by a decimal. This is because 5.64 had been multiplied by only 7 tenths.

Here is an unusual example:

$$0.39 \times$$
$$0.12$$
$$\overline{0.0468}$$

(Check this sum on a calculator but be careful to put the decimal point in the correct place.)

23 18.4 × 6	**24** 23.31 × 5	**25** 13.6 × 0.7
26 £8.24 × 9	**27** £12.28 × 6	**28** £1.25 × 4
29 £135.27 × 8	**30** £72.26 × 13	**31** £45.06 × 22
32 £85.24 × 2.5	**33** £5.28 × 125	**34** £2.50 × 102
35 3.284 kg × 4	**36** 2.04 litre × 6	**37** 8.250 m × 12
38 $1.86 × 8.5	**39** Francs 9.60 × 17	**40** DM2.86 × 25

41 18 gallons @ £2.26 per gallon

42 42 litres @ £0.48 per litre

43 16.25 kg @ £1.02 per kg

Quick methods

$$25.84 \times 10 \quad = \quad 258.4$$
$$92.371 \times 100 \quad = \quad 9237.1$$
$$48.26 \times 1000 = 48260$$

Note that the decimal point is moved one place to the right when multiplying by 10, two places when multiplying by 100, three places when multiplying by 1000 and so on.

$$£24.63 \times 10 \quad = \quad £246.30$$
$$£1.27 \times 1000 = £1270$$
$$\$1.75 \times 100 \quad = \$175$$

Use the quick method to work out these questions:

44 £18.25 × 10	**45** £106.42 × 100	**46** £0.75 × 1000
47 DM2.75 × 100	**48** $1.72 × 1000	**49** Yen 255.5 × 10
50 47.285 kg × 100	**51** 42.65 litres × 10	**52** 4.258 × 1000

– 4 –

Division

1	36 ÷ 12	**2**	63 ÷ 7	**3**	24 ÷ 3	**4**	56 ÷ 8
5	72 ÷ 9	**6**	132 ÷ 11	**7**	72 ÷ 6	**8**	35 ÷ 5
9	60 ÷ 12	**10**	81 ÷ 9	**11**	48 ÷ 4	**12**	28 ÷ 7
13	121 ÷ 11	**14**	18 ÷ 3	**15**	42 ÷ 7	**16**	96 ÷ 8

Using the tables:

17	738 ÷ 6	**18**	1377 ÷ 9	**19**	2325 ÷ 5
20	203 ÷ 7	**21**	418 ÷ 11	**22**	4140 ÷ 12
23	33648 ÷ 8	**24**	13300 ÷ 4	**25**	1536 ÷ 6
26	1625 ÷ 25	**27**	4026 ÷ 33	**28**	6832 ÷ 122

A common error in division is to forget to include the 0 in the answer to the following type of example:

$$8{\overline{\smash{\big)}\,9648}} \quad = 1206$$

29	812 ÷ 4	**30**	2010 ÷ 5	**31**	6072 ÷ 12

In decimal division the following rules should be observed:

a First place the decimal point in the answer space vertically above the decimal point in the question, e.g.

$$8{\overline{\smash{\big)}\,17.04}}$$

then divide

$$8{\overline{\smash{\big)}\,17.04}} \quad = 2.13$$

32	4.92 ÷ 4	**33**	9.624 ÷ 8	**34**	81.6 ÷ 12

b *Do not* divide by a decimal (unless you are using a calculator), e.g.

$$2.4{\overline{\smash{\big)}\,3.744}}$$

Multiply both the divisor (2.4) and the dividend (3.744) by 10 and the sum now becomes:

$$24{\overline{\smash{\big)}\,37.44}}$$

and the answer

$$24\overline{)37.44} \quad {}^{1.56}$$

Similarly

$$0.25\overline{)3.275}$$

becomes

$$25\overline{)327.5} \quad \text{(by multiplying by 100)}$$

35 $1.62 \div 0.6$ **36** $4.56 \div 0.12$ **37** $41.75 \div 0.025$

c By adding 0 to any remainder and dividing again, a more accurate answer can be obtained, e.g.

(i)
$$5\overline{)34.26}$$

$$5\overline{)34.260} \quad {}^{6.852}$$

(ii) Depending upon how accurate you need an answer you can add more noughts, e.g.

$$8\overline{)35.1}$$

$$8\overline{)35.1000} \quad {}^{4.3875}$$

38 $12.3 \div 5$ **39** $34.1 \div 4$ **40** $28.3 \div 8$

Sometimes an answer is required worked out to a certain number of places after the decimal point, e.g.

$$8\overline{)35.1}$$

Give the answer to 2 decimal places

Answer

$$8\overline{)35.10} \quad {}^{4.38}$$

Ignore any remainder (in this case 6) after 2 decimal places.

41 $181.5 \div 8$ (answer to 2 decimal places)

42 $23.53 \div 6$ (answer to 3 decimal places)

43 $14.8 \div 7$ (answer to 2 decimal places)

A more accurate answer can be obtained by *correcting* to a given number of decimal places, e.g.

Express 14.247 corrected to 2 decimal places

Method

Look at the figure in the third decimal place and if the figure is a five or higher value (in this case it is 7) then add 1 to the value of the figure in the second decimal place. If the figure is lower than 5, leave the figure in the second place unchanged.

14.247 corrected to 2 decimal places is 14.25

Remember: examine the figure in the second decimal place if you are correcting to 1 decimal place, examine the figure in the third decimal place if you are correcting to 2 decimal places and so on.

Here are more examples

17.2355 corrected to 3 decimal places is 17.236
121.452 corrected to 2 decimal places is 121.45
£517.676 corrected to the nearest penny is £517.68

44 18.271 corrected to 1 decimal place

45 £181.455 corrected to 2 decimal places (nearest penny)

46 14.2238 corrected to 3 decimal places

47 207.28 km corrected to the nearest kilometre

48 17.8 kg corrected to the nearest kg

Quick methods

$$896.8 \div 10 = 89.68$$
$$175 \div 100 = 1.75$$
$$18.29 \div 1000 = 0.01829$$

The decimal place is moved one place to the left when dividing by 10, two places when dividing by 100, three places when dividing by 1000, and so on.

49 $24.28 \div 10$ **50** $£418.76 \div 100$ **51** $516.29 \div 1000$

52 $65 \text{ kg} \div 10$ **53** $820.5 \text{ litres} \div 100$ **54** $450 \text{ m} \div 1000$

— 5 —

Problems using the four rules

1. The A.B.C. travel agency had 176 passengers booked on a visit to London. A coach firm offered the following rates for the trip:

   21 seater coach (2 available) – £100
   48 seater coach (4 available) – £150
   50 seater coach (4 available) – £165
   54 seater coach (3 available) – £175

   What is the best economical combination of coaches and give the total cost?

2. The money collected from the cash kiosk at the dodgems in the fairground was in the following denominations:

   Three £20 notes, Twenty-six £10 notes, Sixty-three £5 notes, Twenty-nine £1 coins, Thirteen 50p, Two hundred and seventeen 20p, One hundred and ninety-five 10p, Forty 5p, Thirty-five 2p, Ninety 1p.

   a   Find the total amount collected
   b   If the commencing float was £20, calculate the number of rides sold at 75p each.

3. The rail fare from Portsmouth to London (return) was £26.20 for adults and £13.10 for children. Calculate the total cost for 2 adults and 3 children.

4. An hotel has 48 double rooms and 30 single rooms. If the charge for a double room is £64 and for a single room is £42, what are total possible takings for rooms in one night?

5. John Atkins earned £2.85 per hour as an attendant at 'The Dive' swimming pool.

   a   What are his gross earnings in a *normal* 37 hour week?
   b   If John received 'time and a half' for any overtime hours, how much would he earn in a week during which he worked 43 hours?

6. A banquet manager was asked to arrange for sherry to be served at the reception for a conference of 142 delegates. Allowing 15 measures (glasses) per bottle of sherry, how many bottles must be ordered? (Allow 1 glass per delegate.)

7. A travel agent was quoted £252 to transport 30 people on an outing. Calculate the lowest price per person the agent could charge to avoid making a loss.

8 a The coffee takings in the Apex Leisure Centre Refreshment Bar amounted to £139.50. How many cups of coffee at 45p each were sold?

b If 1100 cakes were sold in one week, find the takings if each cake was sold at £0.35.

9 The highest temperatures recorded in Rome during July were as follows:

1	2	3	4	5	6	7	8	9
26.5	26	24.2	23	27	27.4	25	25.6	28

10	11	12	13	14	15	16	17	18
27	26.5	22.5	22.8	25	27.5	26.8	24	22.1

19	20	21	22	23	24	25	26	27
20	21	26.6	27.9	29	28.2	27	26.4	26

28	29	30	31
26	28.1	28	25.6

Find the average highest temperature in July.

10 Mr & Mrs Jones decided to take their four nephews and 2 nieces on a trip to the Undersea Life Centre at Northsea. The prices of admission were as follows:

A family ticket (2 adults and 2 children) – £3.75, Adults – £1.50, Children – £0.75.

a What was the total cost of admission?
b What would be the cost if Mr & Mrs Jones took one child?

11 A tour operator arranged for 5 coaches to start from different towns in the United Kingdom en route to different holiday areas in Europe. The coaches were to meet at Dover port where passengers would transfer to the coach taking them to the area of their choice (pre-arranged). On coach C travelling from Cardiff there were 17 out of the 54 tourists seats vacant. The courier noted that 28 passengers would leave the coach at Dover and 33 would get on. At Dover some passengers had left the coach to visit the toilets and/or buy a drink.

a 15 minutes before embarkation the courier found there were 19 empty seats. How many passengers were missing?
b How many passengers from Cardiff remained on coach C all the way to their destination in Europe?
c How many seats on coach C would be vacant when travelling on the continent?

12 The cost in producing a buffet for 75 tourists at the Derwent Leisure Complex were as follows:

Food per person	£3.20
Drinks per person	£1.50

Labour   £91.50
Overheads   £82.86

If the caterers charged £575, calculate the profit.

13 A holiday in Majorca was advertised for £190 per person but one
free place was offered for every 6 paying persons. A group of 8
students decided to take advantage of the offer. If they shared the
total cost, how much would each student pay?

14 Mr & Mrs Brown and their two children booked a week's holiday
in a guest house but Mr & Mrs Green and their two children
rented a self catering apartment. Compare the costs and find the
difference over seven days and nights using the following
information:

Prices at the guest house (for full board)
Adults £15 per night   Children £8.50 per night

Prices for the apartment and food (for four)
Apartment – £200 per week   Food costs – £10 per day

15 A camp site needed to reseed (grass) on an area outside the
reception office. The patch measured 18 metres by 16.75 metres.
If the recommended seed coverage is 50 g per square metre what
weight should be purchased? (Answer to nearest kg.)

— 6 —

Miles and kilometres

In the UK we measure distances between towns in miles but on the
continent of Europe and most other parts of the world distances are
measured in kilometres (km). A kilometre is shorter than a mile and it
is important not to confuse the two units when calculating distances.

To express kilometres in miles, multiply by 0.62.

Example

Express 400 km in miles

Method

$$400 \times 0.62 = 248 \text{ miles}$$

To express miles in kilometres, divide by 0.62.

Example

Express 155 miles in km

Method
$$155 \div 0.62 = 250 \text{ km}$$

(In working out the following questions give your answer to the nearest unit required.)

1   Express 850 km in miles

2   Express 217 miles in km

3   If the distance from Glasgow to Portsmouth is 460 miles, give the distance in km

4   Taking advantage of the autoroute, the distance between Calais and Nice is 1222 km. Give this distance in miles.

5   London is approximately 75 miles from Dover and Paris is approximately 290 km from Calais. Calculate:

   a   How much nearer is London to Dover than Paris is to Calais. Give your answer in km.
   b   The total *driving* mileage from London to Paris.

6   A German tourist visits a tourist office in Dover and enquires about the distance to Manchester. She is told the distance is 260 miles. 'How many kilometres is that?' she asks. What answer should she be given?

Distances by road are often presented in the form of a grid as shown below. Here is a selection of main towns in France with approximate distances between them shown in *kilometres*:

Bordeaux							
870	Calais						
635	460	Cherbourg					
660	855	915	Grenoble				
550	750	810	104	Lyon			
804	1222	1280	334	470	Nice		
580	290	360	565	460	930	Paris	
245	1000	860	535	535	560	706	Toulouse

Example

Find the distance between Lyon and Calais.

Method

Place a rule along the line of figures horizontal with Lyon and trace down the line of figures under Calais until your finger meets the rule at 750 (see shaded area). The distance between Lyon and Calais is 750 km.

7 Find the distance between Paris and Bordeaux.

8 Find the distance between Toulouse and Grenoble.

9 Calculate the distance in *miles* between Nice and Cherbourg.

10 A motorist asks a travel agent to book a passage on the ferry from Dover to Calais on route to Toulouse. He dose not wish to drive further than 250 miles each day and he asks the agent to book evening accommodation along the route.

   a Calculate the total *mileage* in France.
   b Assuming that the motorist leaves Calais at 9.30 a.m. what is the minimum number of night halts that will be required on route?

11 A coach is hired to take a party of holiday makers from Cardiff to Nice. The distance from Cardiff to Portsmouth is 140 miles but the distance from Cardiff to Dover is 255 miles. If the coach averages 8 miles per gallon and fuel costs average £2 per gallon:

   a calculate the difference in fuel costs (one way) in taking either the Portsmouth/Cherbourg crossing or the Dover/Calais crossing. (Give your answer to the nearest £10.)
   b What other considerations might be taken into account? (Discussion.)

— 7 —

Speed, time and distance

When planning a journey by road it is usual to estimate the time the journey will take. To do this we must work on an average speed – either miles per hour (mph) or kilometres per hour (kph).

Example

A family planned a trip to Edinburgh from their home in Manchester. If the distance to be travelled is 200 miles and it is estimated that an average speed of 40 mph can be maintained. Calculate the expected time to be taken for the journey.

Method

$$\text{Formula to learn: } \frac{\text{Distance}}{\text{Speed}} = \text{Time} \quad (\text{Distance} \div \text{Speed} = \text{Time})$$

therefore: $\dfrac{200}{40} = \text{Time}$

$\qquad\quad = 5 \text{ hours}$

$\qquad\quad = \text{Time taken for the journey.}$

NB If the distance is in *miles* and the speed is in *mph* then the time will be in *hours*.
If the distance is in *kilometres* and the speed is in *kph* then the time will be in *hours*.

1 Calculate the time taken to travel 245 miles at an average speed of 35 mph.

2 Calculate the time taken to travel 325 km at an average speed of 65 kph.

3 John and Jill left Fishguard at 6.30 a.m. to travel the 225 miles to Bournemouth. John reckoned on maintaining an average speed of 30 mph. What was the estimated time of arrival they gave the guest house owner if they intended stopping one hour for lunch?

4 The Derby Theatre Group organised a visit to Stratford-upon-Avon to see a production of 'Macbeth'. The organiser wanted to arrive at the theatre half an hour before the performance began. If the play commenced at 7.15 p.m. what was the latest time the coach could leave Derby if the distance to Stratford was 63 miles and the coach company estimated an average speed of 36 mph?

5 Using the grid on page 12 calculate the actual *driving* time taken from Calais to Toulouse at an average speed of 75 kph.

The hours a coach driver can drive during a day are controlled by law. A driver can not drive for longer than a $4\frac{1}{2}$-hour period before taking a break of at least $\frac{3}{4}$ of an hour. In one day, the total driving time must not exceed 8 hours.

6 A coach leaves Cherbourg at 9.30 a.m., the driver having stayed

the night in a local *pension*.

a What is the latest time he can take a break?
b During the day he makes stops of $1\frac{1}{2}$ hours in total. What is the latest time he must finish driving for the day?

7 The driver of a coach drove for the maximum allowed time during a day in which the coach averaged 35 mph. Calculate the distance travelled by the coach

    a in miles
    b in km.

8 A coach party on route from Cambridge to Exeter planned to stop after 132 miles for lunch at Salisbury and then drive the 89 miles to Exeter in the afternoon.

If the driver estimated the average travelling speed at 30 mph, would the planned journey be possible with one driver?

— 8 —

Maps and plans

It is normally possible to calculate the distances between towns on a map by reading the printed miles or kilometres between points and making a simple addition or subtraction. However, it is sometimes necessary to measure the distance between points on a map (this is best done by using an **opisometer**) and then converting this measurement (probably inches or cm) to miles or kilometres. The map is said to be 'drawn to scale'. For example, a line of length 1 cm may represent 1 km. An architect will use smaller units to show the size of buildings or plots of land.

1 On a scale of 1 inch to the mile, what distance is represented by $3\frac{1}{2}$ inches?

2 On a scale of 1 cm to 5 km, what distance is represented by 3 cm?

3 On a scale of 1 cm to the km, what length on the map represents 12 km?

4 On a scale of 1 cm to the metre, what length is represented by 2 cm?

5 On a scale of 1 cm to the metre, what length is represented by 13.75 cm?

6 Two towns are shown on a map as 2.5 cm apart. Calculate the actual distance between these towns if 1 cm represents 20 km.

Most maps and plans are drawn to scale and the scale should be shown somewhere on the map or plan, possibly on the front cover. The scale of a plan using 1 cm to the metre can be shown as 1 to 100 or, 1:100, because there are 100 cm in 1 metre. In other words, the plan is drawn $\frac{1}{100}$ of the true size.

A map with a scale 1:100 000 means that the real distance between two points is 100 000 times the distance on the map, e.g. 1 cm = 100 000 cms = 1 km.

7   The scale on a plan was shown as 1:200. Calculate the actual length of a football pitch shown as 50 cm on the plan.

8   Using an opisometer, it was found that the distance between two towns on a map was 4.5 cm. Find the actual distance in km if the map was drawn to a scale of 1:200 000.

9   The planners of a leisure centre reckoned that the maximum possible length of a swimming pool could be 30 metres. If a plan was drawn using the scale 1:1000 what measurement would represent the length of the pool?

10   If a map of Germany was drawn to a scale of 1 cm = 2 km, what distance is represented by 5 mm on the map?

11

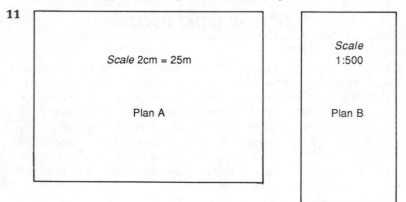

Use a ruler to find the answers.

For plan A find   (i)   the actual length (in metres)
                  (ii)   the actual width
                  (iii) the actual area – length × width.

For plan B find   (i)   the actual length (in metres)
                  (ii)   the actual width
                  (iii) the actual area.

— 9 —

Cancelling

Cancelling makes the working out of fractions and percentages easier and less tedious by simplifying the numbers. For example, two quarters is nearly always referred to as one half.

$$\frac{2}{4} = \frac{1}{2}$$

The value has remained the same by dividing the top *and* the bottom lines by 2. The secret is in finding a number that will divide *exactly* into *both* the top and bottom lines.

Cancel $\dfrac{15}{25}$

$\dfrac{15}{25} = \dfrac{3}{5}$ (by dividing the top and bottom lines by 5)

Cancel the following (always examine your answer in case it will cancel again):

1 $\dfrac{30}{36}$ **2** $\dfrac{40}{45}$ **3** $\dfrac{10}{20}$ **4** $\dfrac{21}{56}$

5 $\dfrac{72}{108}$ **6** $\dfrac{125}{1000}$ **7** $\dfrac{34}{51}$ **8** $\dfrac{4}{12}$

9 $\dfrac{200}{700}$ **10** $\dfrac{16}{64}$ **11** $\dfrac{20\,000}{50\,000}$ **12** $\dfrac{27}{81}$

13 Joanne was carrying out a survey in The Yorkshire Dales. Out of 85 people questioned, she found 17 were from overseas.

    a Show the overseas visitors as a fraction of those questioned.
    b Cancel this fraction and then complete this sentence: One in .... were from overseas.
    c Is the answer to **b** easier to understand and remember than the answer to **a**?

— 10 —

Mixed numbers and improper fractions

Unless you are using a calculator you will not be able to work out percentages without the ability to multiply fractions and that involves mixed numbers and improper fractions.

Example

a   Change $2\frac{1}{3}$ to thirds

Method:

In 2 whole numbers there are 6 thirds (2×3)
Therefore in $2\frac{1}{3}$ there are 7 thirds $= \frac{7}{3}$
$2\frac{1}{3}$ is called a mixed number and $\frac{7}{3}$ is called an improper fraction.

Example

b   Change $6\frac{2}{5}$ to fifths

Method

In 6 whole numbers there are 30 fifths $= \frac{30}{5}$
Therefore in $6\frac{2}{5}$ there are $\frac{32}{5}$

1 Change $1\frac{1}{4}$ to quarters	2 Change $4\frac{1}{2}$ to halves
3 Change $5\frac{1}{6}$ to sixths	4 Change $3\frac{3}{8}$ to eighths
5 Change $2\frac{11}{100}$ to hundredths	6 Change $3\frac{2}{7}$ to sevenths
7 Change 11 to thirds	8 Change $12\frac{3}{4}$ to quarters
9 Change $25\frac{1}{5}$ to fifths	10 Change $2\frac{3}{20}$ to twentieths

Now to change the improper fraction back to a mixed number.

Example

Change the improprer fraction $\frac{11}{4}$ to a mixed number

Method

The fraction $\frac{11}{4}$ means 11 divided by 4
11 divided by 4 = 2 whole numbers, remainder 3 quarters $= 2\frac{3}{4}$

Change to mixed numbers:

11 $\frac{5}{2}$ **12** $\frac{14}{3}$ **13** $\frac{15}{4}$

14 $\frac{21}{8}$ **15** $\frac{40}{7}$ **16** $\frac{100}{9}$

17 $\frac{29}{7}$ **18** $\frac{20}{3}$ **19** $\frac{63}{11}$

20 $\frac{14}{4}$ (cancel first)   **21** $\frac{100}{12}$ (cancel first)   **22** $\frac{42}{12}$ (cancel first)

— 11 —

Multiplication of fractions

Example

a $\frac{2}{3} \times \frac{4}{7}$

Method

Multiply top and bottom lines
$$\frac{2}{3} \times \frac{4}{7} = \frac{8}{21}$$

Example

b $\frac{3}{4} \times \frac{5}{6}$

Method

By cancelling any figure on the top lines with any figure on the bottom lines (if possible) the sum is easier to work out.
$$\frac{^{1}\cancel{3}}{4} \times \frac{5}{\cancel{6}_{2}} = \frac{5}{8}$$

Remember the same number must be divided into the top and bottom lines. (In the above example the division is by 3.)

Example

c $3\frac{1}{2} \times \frac{3}{5}$

Method

First change all mixed numbers to improper fractions and then multiply.
$$\frac{7}{2} \times \frac{3}{5} = \frac{21}{10} = 2\frac{1}{10}$$

Multiply the following:

1 $\frac{2}{3} \times \frac{4}{5}$ **2** $\frac{5}{11} \times \frac{3}{4}$ **3** $\frac{5}{8} \times \frac{5}{6}$

4 $\frac{2}{5} \times \frac{3}{7}$ **5** $\frac{4}{7} \times \frac{1}{2}$ **6** $\frac{2}{5} \times \frac{10}{11}$

7 $\frac{2}{3} \times \frac{3}{4}$ **8** $\frac{5}{6} \times 1\frac{1}{4}$ **9** $2\frac{2}{3} \times \frac{2}{5}$

10 $2\frac{1}{2} \times 1\frac{1}{4}$ **11** $1\frac{1}{2} \times 1\frac{2}{3}$ **12** $4\frac{2}{7} \times 3\frac{1}{2}$

13 $2\frac{2}{5} \times 3$ (write as $\frac{3}{1}$) **14** $2\frac{2}{3} \times 5$

15 $6 \times \frac{3}{4}$ **16** $7 \times \frac{3}{4}$

17 Find $\frac{2}{3}$ of $\frac{1}{4}$ ($\frac{2}{3} \times \frac{1}{4}$) **18** Find $\frac{3}{4}$ of $2\frac{5}{6}$

19 Find $\frac{1}{100}$ of $\frac{25}{28}$ **20** Find one third of three quarters

— 12 —

Percentages – expressing one amount as a percentage of another

Price reductions, commission, occupancy, fare increases, surcharges, wage increases, inflation, mortgages – you will have seen all these expressed in terms of percentages.

It is so much easier to refer to a *percentage* increase from 12% to 15% than a fraction increase from $\frac{3}{25}$ to $\frac{3}{20}$ – yet they are the same.

Example

a Express £3 as a % of £4.
As a fraction it would be shown as $\frac{3}{4}$. To express a fraction as a percentage multiply by 100.

Method

$\frac{3}{4} \times \frac{100}{1} = 75\%$

Example

b Express £9.60 as a % of £16.00.
   (When any one amount contains pence, change both amounts to pence.)

Method

$$\frac{960}{1600} \times \frac{100}{1} = 60\%$$

Example

c Asking a question in a different way, what % of £2000 is £75?

Method

$$\frac{75}{2000} \times \frac{100}{1} = \frac{15}{4} = 3.75\%$$ (by dividing the bottom into the top line)

1   Express 75 as a % of 250

2   Express £42 as a % of £168

3   Express 80p as a % of £2.00

4   Express £3.75 as a % of £150.00

5   Express $14 as a % of $84

6   Express $5.25 as a % of $10.00 (change to cents)

7   Express 4 kg as a % of 6.250 kg (change to g)

8   Express £3500 as a % of £20 000

9   Express 250 F as a % of 2250 F

10 Express 3 litres as a % of 3 litres 750 millilitres

11 What % of 180 is 135?

12 What % of 110 is 90?

13 What % of £25 is £18.50?

14 What % of £2.00 is £0.08?

15 What % of $15 is $10?

16 What % of £5000 is £125?

17 What % of 10 kg is 8.255 kg?

18 What % of 518 is 259?

19 What % of 18 metres is 13.5 metres?

20 What % of £27.50 is £5.50?

— 13 —

Percentage problems

1   A 250 seater aircraft left Gatwick with 20 seats vacant. What percentage of the seats were occupied?

2   A tour operator needed 80% occupancy of an hotel in Majorca to break even (cover her costs). If the hotel offered 175 beds and the operator sold 150, would the operator break even?

3   The Westhaven putting green increased the price per round from 75p to 80p. What was the percentage increase on the original price.

4   Jane worked at the Witchester Tourist Information Office where she was paid £2.95 per hour for a 35 hour week. The hourly wage rate was increased to £3.10.

Calculate:

a the percentage increase in the hourly rate.
b the gross increase in money Jane would receive per week.

5   Increased aviation fuel cost meant a surcharge of £18.75 on a holiday originally priced at £375. Find the percentage increase.

6   During the second week in March 2800 people attended the Quick Dip Swimming Pool and the takings amounted to £2240. A survey one year later revealed that 2590 attended during the second week in March and the takings were £2201.50.

Find:

a The percentage drop in attendance from one year to the next.
b The percentage increase or decrease in the price charged in the second year.

7   During one year the number of holidays sold by a travel agency were as follows:

     Self Catering – 1825   Hotel   – 1570
     Cruises   – 850   Travel only – 1200

     Calculate each type of holiday as a percentage of the total.

8   A bottle of wine purchased on a cross channel ferry cost £3.05. The same wine purchased in a wine shop in the UK cost £3.45. Express the difference in the price as a percentage of:

a The ferry price
b The wine shop price

9   Of the 2340 people making use of a leisure complex in one week, it was found that 1521 were male. What percentage of attenders were female?

10   A camp site was divided as follows:

     Tents – 45 pitches,
     Touring caravans – 52 pitches,
     Static caravans – 36 pitches.

What percentage of the site was reserved for touring caravans?

— 14 —
Gross profit (g.p.)

Profit is generally referred to as either *Gross Profit* or *Net Profit*. The term gross profit is widely used in industries such as the Hotel and Catering industry and denotes the difference between the buying and selling price of an item.

Example

a The selling price of a meal is £9.00 but the food cost in providing the meal is £3.00. Find the Gross Profit.

Method

Selling Price	£9.00
Cost Price	£3.00
Gross Profit	£6.00

The Gross Profit is usually expressed as a percentage of the selling price.

$$\frac{6}{9} \times \frac{100}{1} = 66.66\%$$

The Gross Profit is 66.66% of the selling price.

Example

b A tour operator advertises a holiday for £280 but the operator has direct costs as follows:

Accommodation – £140   Air fare – £98.

Find the Gross Profit and express this profit as a percentage of the advertised price.

Advertised price	£280 (selling price)
Operator's costs	£238
Gross Profit	£42

Gross Profit = $\frac{42}{280} \times \frac{100}{1} = 15\%$ of the advertised price.

Sometimes the retailer will express the profit as a percentage of costs.

Example

c A travel agent sold a holiday for £528 but airline and accommodation costs accounted for £480.

Express the Gross Profit as a percentage of the *costs*.

Selling price	£528
Costs	£480
Gross Profit	£48

$$\text{Gross Profit} = \frac{48}{480} \times \frac{100}{1} = 10\% \text{ of } Costs.$$

(Ignore the effect of Value Added Tax in the following questions.)

1 A travel agency advertised a holiday for £360. This price covered the agent's costs of accommodation – £210, airfare – £120, insurance – £12. Calculate the Gross Profit as a percentage of the advertised price.

2 A restaurant bought a bottle of wine for £2.60 and sold it for £6.50. Find the Gross Profit as a percentage of the selling price.

3 The Fly Away travel shop sold an airline ticket for £300. If Fly Away paid £273 to the airline, calculate the Gross Profit made by the travel shop.

4 A fishing club decided to charge £6.50 per member for a day's fishing off the coast. The 48 seater coach cost £150, the boat cost £85 and the packed lunch cost £1.10 per person.

Find:

a the Gross Profit for increasing club funds if all 48 seats were sold.
b the financial situation if 40 seats were sold.

5 The Relaxe Leisure Centre charged £2.50 per person for an afternoon tea dance. On average 90 people attended. Calculate the expected Gross Profit each week if the costs to the Leisure Centre for this dance were: Band – £75, Light refreshment – 80p per person.

6 Calculate a tour operator's Gross Profit as a percentage of turnover if he sold 200 holidays at an average price of £425 and he received invoices of £30 000 from airlines and £38 000 from the hotels and guest houses.

7 A cut price air ticket office sold a return flight to Tokyo for £750. If the airline charged £700 for the ticket what was the Gross Profit received by the ticket office expressed as a percentage of the *payment to the airline*.

8 The Sea View Hotel charged £14.50 for a five course meal. The food costs were as follows: Meat – £3.25, Vegetables – £0.85, Sweet – £1.25.

Calculate the Gross Profit as a percentage of the selling price.

— 15 —
Net profit

So far we have only considered the direct costs such as air fares, accommodation and food but there are other important costs that have to be deducted from money received before a final or Net Profit can be calculated. The wages of staff, the cost of the telephone, repairs, power, advertising, and the business rate, all have to be paid out of turnover. These costs can be grouped under two headings – **Labour** and **Overheads**.

- **Labour Costs** include wages, national insurance (paid by the employer), staff turnover (recruitment and training), accommodation and food (usually only relevant for Hotel, Catering and Holiday Camp staff).

- **Overheads** include gas, electricity, telephone, advertising, repairs, insurance (property etc.) business rates, depreciation.

- **Net Profit** is the difference between the price at which goods and services are sold and the **total cost**.

  OR

- **Net Profit** can be found by first finding the **Gross Profit** and then subtracting the **Labour** and **Overheads**.

Example

A tour operator sells a series of holidays for £25 000. The cost involved were as follows:

> Ferry charges – £8500, Accommodation – £11 000, Labour costs £1500, Overheads – £2000.

Find the Net Profit and express the answer as a percentage of the sales.

Method

Ferry & Accommodation	£19 500	Sales	£25 000
Labour	1 500	Total Costs	23 000
Overheads	2 000		
		Net Profit	£2 000
Total Costs	£23 000		

$$\frac{2000}{2500} \times \frac{100}{1} = 8\%$$

Net Profit = 8% of sales

(Ignore the effect of Value Added Tax in the following questions.)

1   A travel agent broke down her week's income and expenditure as
    follows:

    Receipts – £10 000; Wages & National Insurance – £540;
    Direct Holiday costs – £7250; Overheads – £1400.

    Find:

    a   the Gross Profit
    b   the Net Profit
    c   the Net Profit as a percentage of the receipts.

2   The books of the Highcliff Caravan Park showed the following
    statistics for September:

    Income from touring caravans – £2750; Income from static
    caravans – £1480; Labour costs – £2040; Overheads – £1925.

    Find the Net Profit for September and express your answer as a
    percentage of the total income.

3   At the end of November the manager of a travel agency produced
    the following results for the month:

    Total holiday sales – £9125; Direct holiday costs – £8175;
    Wages, etc. – £805; Overheads – £650.

    a   Work out the final position for November showing any profit
        or loss as a percentage of sales.
    b   Suggest a reason for your answer to a. (For discussion)

4   Study these details taken from the books of a travel operator:

    Turnover from holiday sales – £175 500; Airline costs –
    £22 000; Ferry costs – £10 450; Hotel accommodation costs –
    £88 000; Labour costs – £8750; Telephone – £2050; Repairs
    and Renewals – £750; Business rate – £1900; Advertising and
    marketing – £23 000; Electricity – £970; Depreciation –
    £1250.

    Calculate:

    a   the Gross Profit
    b   the Net Profit
    c   the Net Profit as a percentage of turnover
    d   the advertising and marketing as a percentage of turnover.

5   If the total costs in one year amounted to 92% of turnover, give the
    Net Profit as a percentage of turnover.

6   The managing committee of the Framley Golf Course had
    budgeted (planned) for a Net Profit of 15% on turnover during a
    12-month period. In fact, the total costs amounted to £1 500 000
    and the income from all sources was £1 750 000.

a What was the actual Net Profit percentage of turnover?
b It was later discovered that £25 000 of members' late subscriptions had not been included in the income. What should the Net Profit percentage have been?

7 The town council of Greathampton thought it prudent to subsidise their tourist office but they expected accounts to be submitted each year. After the first year the following figures were presented:

Income from selling literature, advertising revenue and commission	£48 460
Full-time labour costs	£19 870
Part-time labour costs	£15 580
Estimated overheads	£25 000

a Find the net position at the end of the year.
b Find the subsidy required from the council.
c Why do you think the council would support the tourist office in this way? (For discussion.)

8 The Travel Rite Agency had guaranteed 'no surcharges' on holidays. From sales of 525 holidays the turnover was £237 250 and total expenses were expected to be £226 980. However, a sudden increase in air fuel prices resulted in an average cost of £20 per holiday.

a Calculate the originally *expected* net figure as a percentage of turnover.
b Find the *actual* percentage net figure.
c What does the answer to **b** signify about pricing policies? (For discussion.)

9 A bus company made a net profit of £32 000 on a turnover of £400 000. During the next year new wage rates would increase labour costs by about £2300, overheads were reckoned to rise by £1750 and fuel costs would probably increase by £2050. Calculate the forecasted net profit in the next year if turnover was estimated to rise by £10 000.

— 16 —

More about percentages

In the previous four chapters we have expressed one amount as a percentage of another but sometimes we need to find a percentage of an amount, e.g. find 3% of £175. 1% is one hundredth ($\frac{1}{100}$) and to find one hundredth of an amount we divide it by 100. There are two methods of working out this type of sum and both involve dividing by 100 to find 1% and then multiplying to find the required percentage.

Example

Find 3% of £175

Method I

$$\frac{175}{100} \times 3 = £5.25$$

(Do not forget to cancel where possible – in this case by 25)

Method II

1% of £175 = £1.75 (Quick division by 100)
therefore 3% = £5.25 (Multiply by 3)

Find 1% of the following:

1	£250	2	£5895
3	$645	4	1850 kg
5	£24.50	6	2300
7	Find 2% of £3800	8	Find 3% of $150
9	Find 5% of £160	10	Find 7% of 1500 kg
11	Find 20% of £4000	12	Find 25% of 840 km
13	Find 15% of £250	14	Find 32% of $500
15	Find 2% of £58	16	Find 15% of £65
17	Find 12% of 2500	18	Find 35% of 680 Francs
19	Find 18% of 1.25 kg (in grams)	20	Find 60% of 4500
21	Find 3% of £18	22	Find 8% of £126

— 17 —

Commission

Agencies, such as those in the business of travel or insurance, partly or entirely make their money by earning commission. That is, they sell a product or service on behalf of someone else and they are paid a sum of money for so doing. Some employees such as hairdressers are paid a commission on the amount of money they earn for their employers.

1   The A.B.C. Travel Agency sold holidays worth £42 000 on behalf of Auto Holidays. Calculate the money received by the agency if Auto Holidays paid 12% of the value of the holidays in commission.

2   The Get Away Travel Shop in Bywater booked a round-the-world flight for a student. The flight cost £1250 and the airline paid the Travel Shop 9% of the cost of the ticket in commission. How much did the airline pay?

3   Jane worked in the ice cream parlour of the Apex Leisure Centre and earned £3.00 per hour for a 35-hour week. In an attempt to increase sales, Jane's employers offered her, in addition to her basic wage, a commission of 2% on all sales over £4000 per week.

   Calculate Jane's total earnings in a week in which she took £4800 in ice cream sales.

4   The Triang Travel Agency booked a group of local businessmen on a Heathrow to Manchester flight for which the total cost was £1060. If the agreed rate of commission for such a booking was 7%, calculate the amount of money received by the Triang Agency.

5   The owner of a travel agency had negotiated a commission of 12.5% on all cruises she could sell for a shipping company. Find the commission received during a period in which she sold cruises to the value of £52 000.

6   A stylist working in the hairdressing salon at the Happy Holiday Camp was paid £185 per week plus 3% commission on all money she brought in over £400.

   What were her gross earnings in a week in which she was responsible for £525 worth of business?

7   As an extra service, Mr Brown, a travel agent, offered holiday insurance against cancellation, illness, accident and loss of

personal belongings. A commission of 30% was paid by the insurance company to the agent for all business sold. Find the commission payable on £8340 worth of insurance sold by Mr Brown.

8 Calculate the total income received by a travel bureau which received the following in commission:

>10% on £25 000 worth of holidays sold from the Beeline Brochure
>10% on £18 000 worth of holidays sold from the Escape Brochure
>8% on £5000 worth of business sold on behalf of Tents International
>9% on £14 200 worth of airline tickets
>10% on £10 400 worth of ferry bookings
>25% on £1250 worth of insurance.

9 A tourist office received 5% commission on all tickets sold for shows and 9% for all coach tours. Find the total received if the office sold tickets for shows to the value of £650 and booked coach tours to the value of £930.

10 What is the difference between a tip and a commission given to a hairdresser?

11 Thames Travel had arranged car hire to the value of £2000 as an agent of Drive-Away Cars and received 25% commission for this service. If Thames Travel collected all monies for car hire, what amount should they send to Drive-Away Cars after deducting their commission?

— 18 —

Discount

The practice of discounting the price of goods, whether they are washing machines, furniture, holidays, airline tickets or cars means taking money away from the original price. It is a method of reducing the price in order to sell items or to get payment quicker.

The discount is usually shown as a percentage. You have probably seen advertisements such as – 'All holiday prices slashed by 5%'.

If the original price of a holiday was £350 and 5% was 'slashed' off that figure, then the new price would be found as follows:

> Original price £350
> 1%   =   £3.50
> 5%   =   £17.50
> Therefore new price is £350 − £17.50   = £332.50.

If you prefer you could say the new price is 95% of the original price −

> 95% of £350 = £332.50

− but this method is best used with a calculator.

Here is another use of the term discount:

> 'Our terms are 2% cash discount if payment is made within one month'.

In other words you may deduct 2% off the bill if you pay within one month. It is an encouragement to pay the bill promptly.

1   A travel agency offered a holiday for £400 but if 6 or more persons booked together then a discount of 4% would be allowed off the price. Calculate the total cost of a holiday for a party of 8 persons.

2   The Carlton Tennis Club received an invoice for £320 for tennis balls which had been delivered the week before. The terms on the invoice stated that if payment was made within 2 weeks a cash discount of 5% could be deducted. What should be the value of the cheque sent off in payment by return of post?

3   A bucket shop offered airline tickets at a discount of 6%. Give the price charged for a ticket normally priced at £250.

4   The price of a villa in Italy was £960 per week but this price was discounted by 20% if the villa was taken between 2 October and 5 April. Calculate the price of two weeks in February.

5   A caravan manufacturer advertised a discount of 15% off the price of its range of caravans at the end of a calendar year.

    a   What is the price of a caravan originally costing £6250?
    b   Why might a caravan manufacturer take this action? (For discussion.)

6   An hotel offered a weekend (Friday night and Saturday night) with normal prices discounted by 30%. Calculate the price for a weekend for a husband and wife if the usual price was £45 per person per night.

7   A waxworks charging £2.50 per entry offered a discount of 15% for parties of 10 or more. Find the total price paid by a group of 12 persons.

8   The price of accommodation at the Playland Holiday Camp was £110 per person per week with a 25% discount for children. Calculate the cost of two weeks holiday at Playland for Mr & Mrs Derby and their two children.

— *19* —

Currency conversion

If £1 sterling, 1 dollar, 1 deutchmark, etc. all had the same value then there would be no need to be able to convert one currency to another. Unfortunately the values change almost every day due to the 'strength' of one nation's currency against another's. This 'strength' is brought about by the movement of money from one country to another which, in turn, is affected by differing interest rates, and imports and exports (including Tourism). Tourists can gain or lose by the change of rates as you will see when working through this chapter.

Let us assume throughout this chapter, unless stated otherwise, that the currency exchange rates are as follows:

Exchange rates for £1 Sterling

Austria (Schillings)	20.55
France (Francs)	9.85
Germany (Deutchmarks)	2.93
Greece (Drachmei)	292.00
Italy (Lira)	2210.00
Spain (Pesetas)	183.25
Switzerland (Francs)	2.46
United States (Dollars)	1.95

Example

a How many Pesetas can be obtained for £100?

Method

If £1 = 183.25 pesetas
then £100 = 183.25 × 100 pesetas
= 18 325 pesetas

NB   To change £s to foreign currency always multiply the rate by the number of £s.

Example

b How many £s can be obtained for 6000 French francs?

Method

If £1 = 9.85 French francs

then 6000 fr. $= \dfrac{6000}{9.85}$ pounds sterling (6000 ÷ 9.85)

$$= £609.13 \text{ (to 2 decimal places)}$$

NB   To change foreign currency to £s always divide the amount of foreign currency by the rate.

As the exchange rates are such awkward amounts, it is suggested you use a calculator to work out the following questions. (Ignore commission unless stated.)

1   How many lira can be obtained for £70?

2   Change $500 to the equivalent value in £s.

3   A Swiss agency quoted a trip on Lake Geneva as 50 Swiss francs. Give this quote in £s.

4   An Austrian tourist arrived at Gatwick with 2000 schillings which he wished to exchange. How many pounds sterling would he receive from the Bureau de Change?

5   A British holidaymaker in a French market was comparing the prices of vegetables with English varieties. She found that the price of tomatoes worked out at about 6 francs per lb. Approximately, how many pence is that per lb?

6   A British tourist in Paris wished to change £60 into French francs. How many francs would he receive?

7   A traveller had returned from a tour round Europe and he ended with the following amounts of foreign money:

      80 Swiss Francs, 100 Austrian Schillings,
      50 French Francs, 5000 Italian Lira.

Calculate the total value in £s working to 2 decimal places of a £.

To pay for the facility of exchanging foreign currency, banks, building societies, travel agencies and bureau de change use one of two methods.

A commission may be charged.

Example One

A bank charged a commission of 1% on all travellers cheques transactions. Calculate the total amount paid by Mr Robertson who ordered travellers cheques to the value of £450.

Value of travellers cheques	£450.00
1% commission	£4.50
Total to pay	£454.50

An exchange bureau may 'buy' foreign money at one
rate and 'sell' foreign money at a different rate (lower).

Example Two

A bureau de change offers to buy French francs at 10
francs to the £ and sell at 9.4 francs to the £.

For £100 a tourist leaving the UK would receive 940
francs *but* for 940 francs a returning tourist would
receive only £94 (940 ÷ 10).

The difference between the buying and selling price (£6)
represents the charge made for the service.

8 An hotel agreed to change a 1000 dollar travellers cheque.
Calculate the amount given in £s if the hotel deducted 2%
commission.

9 A travel agency charged the following rates of commission:

   1% on travellers cheques, 2% on cash transactions.

Find the total in £s received by a German tourist who presented
500 deutchmarks in travellers cheques and 50 deutchmarks in
cash.

10 The notice board advertising exchange rates stated that a bank
bought Italian lira at 2300 to the pound and sold lira at 2155 to
the pound.

   a The first person in the queue presented £100 to exchange for
   lira. How many lira would he receive?
   b The second person presented 215 500 lira to exchange for £s.
   How many £s would she receive?
   c If the above two people had exchanged their money outside
   the bank at 2155 lira to the pound, how much better off
   would the second person be (to nearest £)?

11 A French traveller presented the receptionist at the Hotel
Splendid with six 100 franc notes in payment of a bill for £56.
The receptionist accepted the notes and gave the change in
British money. Find the change given (to nearest penny).

12 A bank offered to buy US dollars at 2.08 and sell at 1.95 to the £.
Calculate the £s an American tourist would receive for $500.

13 The notice above the bank clerk stated 'Swiss francs bought at
2.65 and sold at 2.46 to the £'.

   Calculate: a the Swiss francs obtained for £1000
               b the £s obtained for 2500 Swiss francs.

— *20* —

Percentage puzzles

Example

a   If £14 is 2% of an amount of money, what is 1%?

Method

If   £14 = 2%

Then $\frac{14}{2} = 1\%$ (This is a simple but
                                            important step to understand.)

Therefore £7.00 = 1%

Example

b   If $30 is 6% of an amount find 1%

Method

If $30 = 6%

Then $\frac{30}{6} = 1\%$
Therefore $5.00 = 1%

1   If £25 = 5% find 1%   2   If £80 = 16% find 1%

3   If 36 francs = 3% find 1%   4   If 40 kg = 8% find 1%

5   If £400 = 20% find 1%

More Examples

c   If £14 is 2% of an amount find 9%

Method

If   £14 = 2%

Then $\frac{14}{2} = 1\%$

Therefore $\frac{14}{2} \times \frac{9}{1} = 9\%$

                = £63

d If £14 = 2% of an amount, find the whole amount (100%)

Method

$$\frac{14}{2} = 1\%$$

$$\frac{14}{2} \times \frac{100}{1} = 100\%$$

$$= £700 \text{ (the whole amount)}$$

6 If £10 is 5% of an amount, find 8%

7 If $42 is 7% of an amount, find 3%

8 If 28 kg is 4% of an amount, find 26%

9 If £39 is 13% of an amount, find 100%

10 If 18 litres is 9% of an amount, find the whole amount.

11 If $81 is 18% of an amount, find 20%

12 If £15 represents the 10% commission collected, find the original amount.

13 If £12 discount was a reduction of 15%, find the original amount.

14 4.5 litres represents an absorption of 12% of cooking oil. Calculate the total amount before absorption.

15 806 members of a golf club were males and this was 65% of the membership. What was the total membership?

16 A travel agency negotiated an 8% reduction on the entrance fee to a zoo for a party of 90 schoolchildren. If the total saving was £12.60, calculate the usual price per child.

– 21 –

Setting a price

There have been occasions over the past few years where travel agencies, tour operators, catering establishments and leisure centres have had difficulty operating within their budgets. Some have been forced to go out of business.

Quite often the prices these establishments are charging are insufficient to cover their *total costs*. It is therefore vital that a realistic and attainable price is fixed for the services they offer. Merely to undercut a competitor without calculating whether the business can afford the lower charge is asking for trouble. To advertise 'No Surcharges' can be foolhardy unless there is a cast-iron guarantee that costs will not rise – an unusual situation.

There are two mathematical methods of setting a price and both involve first calculating the costs to be covered.

'A' | *Formula to Learn*   *Costs + Profit = Selling Price (100%)* |

Example

The total costs of a holiday were £270. If the Tour Operator worked on a Net Profit of 10% on turnover (sales), at what price should the holiday be offered?

Method

Cost + Profit (10%) = Selling Price (100%)
Therefore the cost = 90% (100% − 10%)
Or £270 = 90%

Then $\dfrac{270}{90} = 1\%$

And $\dfrac{270}{90} \times \dfrac{100}{1} = 100\%$ (selling price)

£300 = selling price of holiday

1   Calculate the price at which a holiday should be offered if the total costs amount to £639 and the Holiday Planner required a Net Profit of 10% on the selling price.

2   A tour operator worked on a Net Profit of 15% on turnover. What price should be set for a holiday with total costs of £1275?

3   The estimated running costs of the Dolphin Swimming pool were £440 000. Calculate the expected receipts if the organising committee expected a Net Profit of 12% on takings.

4   A ferry company issued a directive to the catering manager that a Gross Profit of 60% on the selling price was required on all food sold on board their ships. Find the price that should be charged for:

a   A salad with a food cost of £2.50
b   A roast with a food cost of £4.05 (to the nearest penny)

5 The proprietor of a coach hire company expected a profit of 20% on income. What quote would he give for a journey where the estimated costs were £45 (to nearest £)?

'B'   Many smaller retail businesses calculate the price by 'Marking Up', that is by adding a percentage to the costs. Because these costs would normally not include labour and overheads, great care has to be taken to use a sufficiently high 'mark up' (for discussion).

Example

A travel agent costed out a holiday at £140. Her policy was to 'mark up' these costs by 10% to find the selling price to the client. At what price was the holiday offered?

Method

Cost	£140
Mark up	£14 (10% of £140)
Offered Price	£154

You could find 110% of £140 to calculate the answer £154. This is a better method if you are using a calculator. Try both when working out the following:

6 The cost of a tour arranged by a travel agent was £210 per person. Calculate the price advertised by the agent if a mark up of 10% was to be added.

7 Mark up £405 by 15% and give your answer to the nearest £.

8 A ski shop was invoiced for £85 for a pair of ski boots. Find the price the shop charged for these boots if the mark up was 25%.

9 A travel agent put together an individual (custom built) holiday with costs per person as follows:

Air Fare	£110
Accommodation	£400
Car Hire	£86
Insurance	£45
Sightseeing	£8

The agent worked on a mark up of 15% on costs. Calculate:

a The price charged per person to the nearest £.
b The total profit if 20 holidays were sold. (Use your answer to **a** to work this out.)

10 A souvenir shop bought 500 small trinkets at 25p each. Find the price charged per trinket by the shop if the mark up was 40%.

11 Two travel agencies had differing pricing policies. Agent A marked up costs by 20% but Agent B preferred to aim for a profit of 15% on sales. Calculate the price charged by both agencies for a holiday with costs of £250 (answer to the nearest £).

12 A travel agent was approached by a college lecturer and asked to quote for a skiing holiday abroad for 30 staff and students. The costs were found to be as follows (exclusive of insurance):

Coach	£550
Accommodation	£4500
Ferry	£750

a Work out the quotation allowing for a 15% mark up.
b What was the total profit?

13 A travel shop calculated the cost of a holiday to be £365 and marked the cost up by 20%. In advertising this holiday the travel shop guaranteed 'No Surcharges'. Twenty five holidays were sold when an increase in fuel prices resulted in the air fare increasing by £20 per ticket.

a What was the original total projected profit?
b By how much was the projected profit reduced by the fare increase?

— 22 —
Days inclusive

It is essential when deciding on insurance cover, return travel dates, car hire periods, lengths of holiday etc. to be able to determine accurately the number of days involved. The term 'inclusive' is important in this respect. Saturday to Saturday inclusive would involve 8 days.

Example

A family booked a holiday commencing 8 July, returning home 22 July. Find the number of days involved inclusive of the travelling days.

Method

$22 - 8 = 14$ (Subtraction of dates)
$14 + 1 = 15$ (inclusive of the last travelling day)

Proof

Days in July involved:

8, 9, 10, 11, 12, 13, 14, 15, 16, 17, 18, 19, 20, 21, 22 = 15 days.

NB One day must be added to the subtraction $(22 - 8)$ when calculating inclusive days.

1 Calculate the number of days between 13 March 1992 and 29 March 1992 inclusive.

2 A holiday insurance company quoted cover by the day. Mr & Mrs Jones left their home to travel to France on Friday 9 June and returned home on Friday 30 June. How many days should be covered?

3 A coach company specified that their return tickets were valid over 10 days. Mary White wished to travel outward on 8 May. State the latest possible return date.

4 A holiday commenced on 31 May and ended 7 June.

a Give the length of the holiday in days inclusive.
b How many nights accommodation were required?

Extra care is required when calculating days involving more than one calendar month. You must know the number of days in each month.

Example

a A holiday was booked from 25 June to 18 July. Give the length of the holiday in days inclusive.

Method

Days in June $(30 - 25) + 1 = 6$
Days in July $\qquad\qquad\quad 18$

Total 24 days

Example

b A cruise left Southampton on 10 January 1991 and returned on 10 March 1991. Calculate the number of inclusive days.

Method

January $(31-10) + 1 = 22$ days
February $\qquad\qquad = 28$ days
March $\qquad\qquad\quad = 10$ days

Total 60 days

5 Find the number of days the Black family must take out overseas insurance on their car (Green Card), if they leave home on 23 August to catch the 10 a.m. ferry on the same day and return to the UK on the 11 a.m. ferry from Calais on 3 September.

6 Camping Britain reserved 5 pitches on the Camping Forest site in the Jura from 15 June until 20 September inclusive. Calculate the number of days the site was booked.

7 Northsea town council charges £2100 per day or part of a day for a fairground site at the edge of town. Calculate the fee received from a fair which moved on site on 29 October and left on 6 November.

8 The terms of a car hire firm were: £25 per day for a particular model, plus 20p per mile. No charge was made for the day if a car was returned by 9 a.m. Find the total hire cost if a hirer picked up a car on 26 February 1992 and returned it at 5 p.m. on 4 March 1992 having driven 450 miles.

9 A caravan site allowed caravans on site after midday on the day of arrival and expected the site to be vacated by midday on the day of departure. The nightly fees were: £3 per site, £1 per adult, £0.50 per child. Calculate the total cost for Mr & Mrs Shepherd and their 3 children if they arrived on site at 3 p.m. on 23 August and departed at 9.30 a.m. on 3 September.

– 23 –

Twenty-four hour clock

Most time tables use the twenty four hour clock because this system helps to prevent confusion over arrival and departure times. It is also easier to add and subtract times using this method.

Here are a few examples showing the same time for the 12 hour and 24 hour system.

12 Hour	24 Hour
8 a.m.	08.00
10.45 a.m.	10.45
2 p.m.	14.00
11.30 p.m.	23.30

In the 24 hour system all times are calculated from midnight and all times are shown using four figures (two figures for hours and two figures for minutes). Sometimes the word 'hours' is written after the figure, e.g. 15.30 hours.

Change the following to the 24 hour clock system:

1	7 a.m.	**2**	9 p.m.	**3**	12.45 p.m.	**4**	4.25 a.m.
5	3.25 p.m.	**6**	Midday	**7**	11.55 p.m.	**8**	1 a.m.

Change the following to the 12 hour system:

9	04.00	**10**	13.30	**11**	17.50	**12**	00.05
13	18.27	**14**	03.10	**15**	21.10	**16**	10.30

17 An hotel receptionist on an evening shift checked her watch at a quarter to seven to log a telephone call. What time would she enter using the 24 hour system?

18 A taxi driver was due to meet the flight arriving Stansted 22.45. He needed to allow $1\frac{1}{2}$ hours for his journey. Using the 12 hour clock give the time he should set out.

19 A travel clerk was explaining to a client the times of a flight from Gatwick to Malta. The plane departed Gatwick 16.40 and arrived Luqa 19.35 (UK time). Using the 12 hour clock, give the information the clerk should have provided.

    a for the departure time.
    b for the arrival time.
    c for the length of the journey.

20 Mr & Mrs Green were meeting their daughter at Heathrow where she was due to arrive at 18.22. The arrivals information showed the expected time of arrival would be 19.05. How late was the flight?

21 The 09.00 ferry from Portsmouth to Cherbourg was time tabled to arrive at 14.45 local time. If the French time was one hour ahead of UK time, calculate the length of the sea crossing.

22 A flight was due to depart Manchester 14.30 and arrive Singapore 05.40 the next day (UK time). Find the length of the journey.

Time zones

At certain times of the year when it is 08.00 in London it is 03.00 in Philadelphia (USA) and 16.00 in Perth (Australia). Why should one town or country be 5 hours behind London and another 8 hours ahead?

Imagine you are in a spacecraft hovering over the North Pole and you look down to see the earth spinning below.

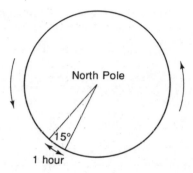

In 24 hours the earth will spin completely round through 360 degrees. Therefore in 1 hour the earth will spin 15° from West to East. (360 ÷ 24)

1   Through how many degrees will the earth spin in 5 hours?

2   Through how many degrees will the earth spin in 12 hours?

3   Is 180° halfway round the earth or three quarters of the way round?

Look at the direction in which the earth spins.

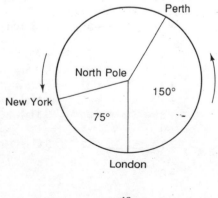

4 If New York is 75° behind London, what time is it there when it is 10.30 in London (ignore dates).

5 If Perth is 150° ahead of London, what time is it there when it is 13.00 in London (ignore dates)?

The degrees are called 'degrees of longitude' and we refer to them as West or East of Greenwich (London) which has been agreed internationally to be 0° longitude. Greenwich sets the standard from which times round the world are calculated – Greenwich Mean Time (GMT).

6 Is New York 75° East or West of London?

7 Is Perth 150° East or West of London?

8 If a country is East of London is the time there behind or ahead of London?

9 If a country is West of London is the time there behind or ahead of London?

10 Lahore (India) is 75° longitude East (approximately). Calculate the time in Lahore when it is midday in London (ignore dates).

Basically the times change by 1 hour for every 15° longitude difference between places but it is sometimes inconvenient for a large country to have many time differences. Imagine how confusing it would be to have differing times in the UK. To simplify the situation, Time Zones have been created so that by referring to tables, the times in different parts of the world can be calculated.

You will find that various countries add or subtract hours at certain periods of the year to make better use of daylight hours (Daylight Saving Time – DST). For instance during the summer months France adds one 'energy saving' hour in an attempt to delay the use of electricity, for lighting, by one hour.

The following table shows some of the time differences round the world during 1990.

Country	Standard Time	DST	DST in Operation
Austria	+1	+2	25 March–29 Sept
Barbados	−4		
Canada (Pacific)	−8	−7	1 Apr–27 Oct
China	+8	+9	15 Apr–15 Sept
Egypt	+2	+3	1 May–30 Sept
France	+1	+2	25 Mar–29 Sept
Greece	+2	+3	25 Mar–29 Sept
Japan	+9		
New Zealand	+12	+13	8 Oct (1989)– 17 Mar (1990)
Singapore	+8		

Country	Standard Time	DST	DST in Operation
Thailand	+7		
UK	GMT	+1	25 Mar–27 Oct
USA (Eastern)	−5	−4	1 Apr–27 Oct
USSR (Moscow)	+3	+4	25 Mar–29 Sept
Yugoslavia	+1	+2	25 Mar–29 Sept

NB   All standard times and Daylight Saving Times are compared to GMT.

Calculating times around the world is quite simple, using the above table.

Example

a When the time in London on 1 August is 15.10, calculate the time in Paris.

Method

On 1 August London is 1 hour ahead of GMT but Paris is 2 hours ahead of GMT.

Therefore Paris is 1 hour ahead of London

The time in Paris must be 16.10 (15.10 + 1 hour).

Because the Paris difference (+2) is greater value than the London difference (+1) then the Paris time must be *ahead* of London.

Example

b When the time in July in Moscow is 14.00 what time will it be in New York?

Method

The difference between Moscow (+4) and New York (−4) is 8 hours.

Therefore the time in New York is 06.00 (14.00 − 8 hours)

Because the Moscow difference (+4) is of a greater value than New York (−4) then Moscow time is ahead of New York.

Calculate the time in each of the following countries using the dates and times shown for the UK.

	Date	UK Time	Country
11	3 Jan	04.00	Egypt
12	18 Mar	21.00	Austria

13	9 July	12.45	Barbados
14	2 Sept	23.30	USA (East)
15	18 Aug	21.00	Japan
16	27 Mar	03.40	Canada (Pacific)

17 When it is 4 a.m. in the UK during July, what time will it be in New Zealand?

18 On 5 March an aircraft leaves Heathrow 18.20 and arrives Vienna 21.30 local time. Calculate the time taken for the flight.

19 On 2 August a businessman in Birmingham must phone New York when the office opens at 8 a.m. What time must he make the call?

20 Graham takes a flight from Tokyo to Gatwick on 25 September. He departs Tokyo 10.10 and spends 50 minutes transferring planes in Seoul. He arrives Gatwick 17.55 UK time. Calculate the actual flying time.

21 Sally had just arrived at Heathrow from a holiday in Athens. The date was 3 July and as her watch showed 3 p.m., she decided to reset it to UK time. What time did she set?

22 In Moscow it was 02.00 on Monday the 14 January. Give the simultaneous time and date details for London.

23 On 2 July a flight departs Glasgow 09.30 and arrives Barbados 15.05 local time. Calculate the flying time.

24 Mr & Mrs Betts were pleasantly surprised to receive a phone call from Bangkok at 4 p.m. on Christmas Day. 'What time is it over there?' Mr Betts enquired. What was their son's reply?

25 Find the time in Athens on 3 July when it is 14.30 in Singapore.

26 At 9.15 a.m. on 23 April a businessman in Saltzburg wishes to phone his associate who will not arrive in his office in Paris until 10 a.m. How long must he wait until he can make the phone call?

27 When the time is 16.55 during August in Egypt, what is the time on the eastern coast of USA?

International Date Line

Of course there must be a point when one day changes to the next, when Monday becomes Tuesday, Tuesday becomes Wednesday and so on.

Although 180° longitude is the opposite side of the world from Greenwich and would be in the position of midnight when it is midday in London – it would be most confusing if the date changeover line passed straight through a town so that in one part it was Monday while in another it was Tuesday. A line has therefore been drawn zigzagging through the Pacific islands so that it avoids areas of population. On the Eastern side of this line it will still be Monday when it is Tuesday on the Western side.

This line is known as the *International Date Line (IDL)*. The diagram below (not drawn to scale) represents the position of New Zealand (+12 hours) and Canada Pacific (−8 hours) on each side of the IDL.

(At 20.00 GMT)
IDL

West	East
New Zealand	Canada (Pacific)
Wednesday 21 March 08.00	Tuesday 20 March 12.00

Earth's spin - - -|- - - - →

NB The relative position of New Zealand, the IDL and Canada never changes. Notice that because the difference between the time in New Zealand and Canada (Pacific) is 20 hours (+12 and −8), when it is 08.00 in New Zealand on Wednesday it is 12.00 on Tuesday in Canada (Pacific).

This helps to explain why you take a day off when you travel from West to East across the IDL and add a day on when you travel from East to West.

28 On Wednesday a cruise liner crosses the IDL from East to West. What new day should be set on the calendars?

29 At midday a plane takes off on Tuesday 1 January 1991 and flies West to East over the IDL. Ten minutes later after crossing the IDL a fishing boat spots the plane and makes a note in the ship's log. Give the day and date details as entered in the log.

25

Reading a timetable and fare table

Timetables and fare tables are a mass of information. A lot of effort has gone into their design in an attempt to present information as simply and clearly as possible. The specimen fare table printed opposite is taken from the 'Car Ferry Guide' of P & O European Ferries. Study the details and you will see there are four tariffs (charge rates). The more popular the crossing time the higher the tariff – this is one way of trying to persuade travellers to use off-peak times. Be sure to read all the relevant conditions.

1 Using tariff D, calculate the cost of a single journey from Portsmouth to Cherbourg for a family of 2 adults and 3 children (ages 4, 6, 10).

2 Find the total cost of a return fare from Portsmouth to Cherbourg using tariff C for 2 adults, 2 children (ages 11, 5) and a car of length 4.95 m.

3 Find the cost of a return journey for 2 adults taking a motorcycle from Portsmouth to Cherbourg under tariff B.

4 The Blount family (2 adults, 3 children ages 5, 7, 9) intend crossing from Portsmouth to Cherbourg. Using a car (length 4.4 m) to tow a caravan (length 5.5 m) they will cross to Cherbourg using tariff C and returning using tariff B. Calculate the ferry fare if they wish to travel Club Class on daylight sailings.

5 Mr & Mrs Robertson book a return passage to Cherbourg during May. They will travel overnight in both directions using a 2 berth cabin and will qualify for tariff D. Find the ferry fare invoiced by their travel agent.

6 During what periods (give dates) is £49 the charge for a Night Sailing 4 berth deluxe cabin?

7 By delaying the times of their ferry crossing a husband and wife with car (length 4.5 m) can travel under tariff E instead of C. How much money would they save on a return journey?

Portsmouth-Cherbourg-Portsmouth

STANDARD SINGLE FARES

	Tariff E £	Tariff D £	Tariff C £	Tariff B £
DRIVERS AND VEHICLE PASSENGERS				
Adults	16.00	19.00	22.00	24.00
Senior Citizens	12.00	16.00	22.00	24.00
Children (4 and under 14) **Children under 4 Free**	8.00	9.00	11.00	12.00
CARS & MOTORCYCLE COMBINATIONS				
Overall length not exceeding 6.50m	42.00	45.00	72.00	86.00
MOTOR HOMES, MOTOR CARAVANS & MINI BUSES				
Overall length not exceeding 6.50m	42.00	45.00	79.00	95.00
10.00m	70.00	76.00	103.00	149.00
TOWED CARAVANS & TRAILERS				
Overall length not exceeding 3.00m	15.00	16.00	28.00	49.00
6.00m	22.00	22.00	35.00	72.00
Additional metre or part thereof	12.00	12.00	12.00	12.00
MOTORCYCLES				
Solo motorcycles, scooters and mopeds	12.00	18.00	20.00	24.00
FOOT PASSENGERS AND CYCLISTS (Cycles free)				
Adults	25.00	25.00	26.00	28.00
Senior Citizens	22.00	23.00	26.00	28.00
Children (4 and under 14) **Children under 4 Free**	12.00	13.00	14.00	14.00

RESERVED ACCOMMODATION

				Low Season £	High Season £
DAY SAILINGS	£	**NIGHT SAILINGS** (2130-2300 hrs) £			
4 berth de luxe cabin with with shower and toilet	22.00	4 berth de luxe cabin/shower/toilet	—	per cabin 49.00	per cabin 66.00
		4 berth cabin	per berth 12.00	per cabin 36.00	per cabin 48.00
4 berth day room	15.00	2 berth cabin	per berth 13.00	per cabin 22.00	per cabin 26.00
2 berth cabin	12.00	Reclining seat (with rug)	3.50		

Cabins and seats on night sailings must be reserved in advance. Low Season: 1 Jan-11 Jul, 2 Sept-31 Dec. High Season: 12 Jul-1 Sept

CLUB CLASS

	Day Sailings	Night Sailings
Club Class	5.00	7.50
Executive Club Class	7.50	—

TERMS AND CONDITIONS

The above fares refer to vehicles for non-commercial use only. Before you book, refer to full conditions, cancellation charges and information on page 33.

The P & O timetable opposite must be used to answer the following questions. The table of time differences round the world on pages 44/45 will enable you to determine arrival times.

Notice the tariff letters used to find the charge for each sailing.

8   How many ferries cross to Cherbourg on 18 May?

9   Using the 12 hour clock give the time the ferry departs Cherbourg to arrive in Portsmouth during the evening in June.

10   Gill Taylor would prefer to arrive in Portsmouth at about midday to catch the first possible ferry to Cherbourg to start her holiday on 14 July and return on the late night ferry on 29 July. She would require a club class seat on the outward journey and a reclining seat on the return journey.

   a   Which sailing should Gill use from Portsmouth?
   b   Which tariff applies (i) from Portsmouth? (ii) from Cherbourg?
   c   Calculate the total cost of the return fares.

11   Find the expected time of arrival in Cherbourg of the 09.00 August sailing using

   a   UK time.
   b   French time.

12   Mr & Mrs Hall (ages 67, 65) will arrive by train at Portsmouth Harbour railway station at 07.30 a.m. on 1 September and will then catch the first available sailing to Cherbourg. Returning from Cherbourg on 25 September they wish to use the daylight sailing. They allow one hour in total at Portsmouth for customs and transport to the railway station.

   a   Give the time of the sailing from Portsmouth.
   b   Which of the following trains should they plan to catch from Portsmouth (assume they wish to catch the first available) – 12.30, 13.00, 13.30, 14.00?
   c   Calculate the total return ferry fares.

13   A group of 8 students plan to drive to Portsmouth in a Mini-bus (length 6 m) on 3 July to catch the 22.30 sailing to Cherbourg and then drive to the South of France. They intend to return by the 23.00 sailing from Cherbourg on 2 August.

   a   Calculate the *total* cost for each student in crossing the channel both ways.
   b   At what time will the ferry reach Cherbourg (local time)?
   c   What is the estimated length of the sea crossing time from Portsmouth to Cherbourg?
   d   Assuming the driving time from the students starting point to Portsmouth is 5 hours – how many days inclusive must their holiday insurance cover?

14 Mr & Mrs Chell, who have one child aged 7 years, went to a travel agency for advice and help in booking a ferry from Portsmouth to Cherbourg. They intended towing a caravan and they lived 3 hours driving time from Portsmouth. They wished to drive a further 50 miles on from Cherbourg on the evening of their arrival. They were happy to commence their holiday on either 10 August or 11 August but they insisted on returning by the first sailing on 1 September. (Car length 4.7 m, Caravan 5.4 m.)

  a Which sailing would you advise if cost had to be kept to a minimum?
  b What would be the total ferry fare quoted by the agency?
  c What time should Mr Chell set on his watch as the ferry docked in Portsmouth at the end of the holiday?

APPROXIMATE SEA CROSSING TIME 4¾ HRS
DAY SAILINGS

(2230 from Portsmouth arrives 0700 next day, 2300 from Cherbourg arrives 0745 next day.)

BUS SERVICES
PORTSMOUTH. A bus service operates between Portsmouth Harbour railway station and the Car Ferry Terminal from March to September. Buses are timed to connect with departure and arrival times.

PORTSMOUTH–CHERBOURG — ALL SAILINGS LOCAL TIMES 1991

```
JAN   T W T F S S M T W T F S S M T W T F S S M T W T F S S M T W T
      1 2 3 4 5 6 7 8 9 10 11 12 13 14 15 16 17 18 19 20 21 22 23 24 25 26 27 28 29 30 31
2230  E E E E E E E E E E E E E E E E E E E E E E E E D E E E E E E E

FEB   F S S M T W T F S S M T W T F S S M T W T F S S M T W T
      1 2 3 4 5 6 7 8 9 10 11 12 13 14 15 16 17 18 19 20 21 22 23 24 25 26 27 28
2230  D E E E E E E D E E E E E E D E E E E E D E E E E E E

MAR   F S S M T W T F S S M T W T F S S M T W T F S S M T W T F S S
      1 2 3 4 5 6 7 8 9 10 11 12 13 14 15 16 17 18 19 20 21 22 23 24 25 26 27 28 29 30 31
0900                                              E E D E E E E E D C D E
2230  D E E E E E E D E E E E E E D E E E E E E E D E E E E

APR   M T W T F S S M T W T F S S M T W T F S S M T W T F S S M T
      1 2 3 4 5 6 7 8 9 10 11 12 13 14 15 16 17 18 19 20 21 22 23 24 25 26 27 28 29 30
0900  E E E E E D E E E E E E D E E E E E D E E E E E E D E E E E
2230  E E E E E E D E E E E E E D E E E E E E D E E E E E E D E E E

MAY   W T F S S M T W T F S S M T W T F S S M T W T F S S M T W T F
      1 2 3 4 5 6 7 8 9 10 11 12 13 14 15 16 17 18 19 20 21 22 23 24 25 26 27 28 29 30 31
0900  E E D D E E E E E E D E E E E E E D E E E E E D C E E E E E D
1300                                              E C C E E E E E D
2230  E D C E E E E E E D E E E E E E D E E E E D C D D D D D C

JUN   S S M T W T F S S M T W T F S S M T W T F S S M T W T F S S
      1 2 3 4 5 6 7 8 9 10 11 12 13 14 15 16 17 18 19 20 21 22 23 24 25 26 27 28 29 30
0900  D C D D D D D D D D D D D D D D D D C D D D D D D D C D C D
1300  D D E E E D D D E E E E E D D D D E E E E D C D D D E E E E D D
2230  D D D D D C D D D D D C D D D D D C D D D D D D D C D D D

JUL   M T W T F S S M T W T F S S M T W T F S S M T W T F S S M T W
      1 2 3 4 5 6 7 8 9 10 11 12 13 14 15 16 17 18 19 20 21 22 23 24 25 26 27 28 29 30 31
0900  D D D D D D D D D D D D D B C C C C C B C C C C C        C C C C
1300  E E E D D D E E E E E C C D D D C C C C B C C C C C B    C C C C
2230  D D D D D D D D C B C D D D D D B C C C C C B C          C C C C

AUG   T F S S M T W T F S S M T W T F S S M T W T F S S M T W T F S S
      1 2 3 4 5 6 7 8 9 10 11 12 13 14 15 16 17 18 19 20 21 22 23 24 25 26 27 28 29 30 31
0900  C B B C C C C C B B C C C C C B B C C C C C B C C C C C D D D D
1300  C C C C C C C B B C C C C C B B C C C C C B C C D D D C C D D D D
2230  B B C C C C C B B C C C C C B B C C C C C B C C C C C C D D D

SEP   S M T W T F S S M T W T F S S M T W T F S S M T W T F S S M
      1 2 3 4 5 6 7 8 9 10 11 12 13 14 15 16 17 18 19 20 21 22 23 24 25 26 27 28 29 30
0900  D D D D D D D D D D D D D D D D D D D D D D D D D D D D D D
1300  D E E E E E E E E E E E E E E E E E E E E E E E E E E E E E
2230  D D D D D C D D D D D D D D D D D C D D D D D D D D D D D D

OCT   T W T F S S M T W T F S S M T W T F S S M T W T F S S M T W T
      1 2 3 4 5 6 7 8 9 10 11 12 13 14 15 16 17 18 19 20 21 22 23 24 25 26 27 28 29 30 31
0900  E E E E D E E E E E E D E E E E E E D E E E E E E D E E E E E
2230  E E E E E D E E E E E E E D E E E E E E D E E E E E E D E E E E

NOV   F S S M T W T F S S M T W T F S S M T W T F S S M T W T F S
      1 2 3 4 5 6 7 8 9 10 11 12 13 14 15 16 17 18 19 20 21 22 23 24 25 26 27 28 29 30
0900  D E E E E E D E E E E E E D E E E E E D E E E E E E D E E E
2230  D E E E E E D E E E E E E D E E E E E D E E E E E E D E E E

DEC   S M T W T F S S M T W T F S S M T W T F S S M T W T F S S M T
      1 2 3 4 5 6 7 8 9 10 11 12 13 14 15 16 17 18 19 20 21 22 23 24 25 26 27 28 29 30 31
0900  E E E E E E E E E E E E E E E E E E E E E E E E E E E E E E E
2230  E E E E E D E E E E E E E D E E E E E E D E E E E E E
```

CHERBOURG–PORTSMOUTH — ALL SAILINGS LOCAL TIMES 1991

```
JAN   T W T F S S M T W T F S S M T W T F S S M T W T F S S M T W T
      1 2 3 4 5 6 7 8 9 10 11 12 13 14 15 16 17 18 19 20 21 22 23 24 25 26 27 28 29 30 31
1700  E E E E E E E E E E E E E E E E E E E E E E E E D E E E E E E E

FEB   F S S M T W T F S S M T W T F S S M T W T F S S M T W T
      1 2 3 4 5 6 7 8 9 10 11 12 13 14 15 16 17 18 19 20 21 22 23 24 25 26 27 28
1700  E E D E E E E E E D E E E E E E D E E E E E E D E E E E

MAR   F S S M T W T F S S M T W T F S S M T W T F S S M T W T F S S
      1 2 3 4 5 6 7 8 9 10 11 12 13 14 15 16 17 18 19 20 21 22 23 24 25 26 27 28 29 30 31
1700  E E D E E E E E E D E E E E E E D E E E E E E E D D E E E
2300                                              E E D D E E E E E D

APR   M T W T F S S M T W T F S S M T W T F S S M T W T F S S M T
      1 2 3 4 5 6 7 8 9 10 11 12 13 14 15 16 17 18 19 20 21 22 23 24 25 26 27 28 29 30
1700  D E E E D D E E E E E D D E E E E E D D E E E E E D D E E
2300  E E E E E E E E E E E E E E E E E E E E E E E E E E E E E E

MAY   W T F S S M T W T F S S M T W T F S S M T W T F S S M T W T F
      1 2 3 4 5 6 7 8 9 10 11 12 13 14 15 16 17 18 19 20 21 22 23 24 25 26 27 28 29 30 31
0800                                              E E E E E E E E
1700  E E E D D C E E E E D D E E E E E E D D E E E E E E E D C D D D
2300  E E E E E D E E E E E E E E E E E E E E E E E E E D D D D D

JUN   S S M T W T F S S M T W T F S S M T W T F S S M T W T F S S
      1 2 3 4 5 6 7 8 9 10 11 12 13 14 15 16 17 18 19 20 21 22 23 24 25 26 27 28 29 30
0800  D D E E E E E D D E E E E E D D E E E E E D D E E E E E D D
1700  C D D D D D C C C C C C C C D D D D D C C C C C D D D D E E E D
2300  D D D D D D D D D D D D D D D D D D C D D D D D D D D D D D

JUL   M T W T F S S M T W T F S S M T W T F S S M T W T F S S M T W
      1 2 3 4 5 6 7 8 9 10 11 12 13 14 15 16 17 18 19 20 21 22 23 24 25 26 27 28 29 30 31
0800  E E E E D D D E E E E E D D D E E E E E D D E E E E E D C D D D
1700  E E E E E E E E E E E E E E E E E E E E E E E E E E E E C C C C
2300  D D D D D D C D D D D D D D C C C C C C C C C C C C C C C C C

AUG   T F S S M T W T F S S M T W T F S S M T W T F S S M T W T F S S
      1 2 3 4 5 6 7 8 9 10 11 12 13 14 15 16 17 18 19 20 21 22 23 24 25 26 27 28 29 30 31
0800  C B B C C C C C B B C C C C C B B C C C C C B B C C C C C D D D
1700  C B B C C C C C B B C C C C C B B C C C C C B B C C C C C D D D
2300  C B C C C C C C B B C C C C C B B C C C C C B B C C C C C D D D

SEP   M T W T F S S M T W T F S S M T W T F S S M T W T F S S M
      1 2 3 4 5 6 7 8 9 10 11 12 13 14 15 16 17 18 19 20 21 22 23 24 25 26 27 28 29 30
0800  B D E E E E E E E E E E E E E E E E E E E E E E E E E E E E
1600                                              E E
1700  C D D D D D D D D D D D D D D D D D D D D D D D D D D D D D E
2300                                              D D

OCT   T W T F S S M T W T F S S M T W T F S S M T W T F S S M T W T
      1 2 3 4 5 6 7 8 9 10 11 12 13 14 15 16 17 18 19 20 21 22 23 24 25 26 27 28 29 30 31
1600  E E E E E D E E E E E E D E E E E E E D E E E E E E D E
1700                                                            D E E E E
2300  E E E D E E E E E E D E E E E E E D E E E E E E E E E E E

NOV   F S S M T W T F S S M T W T F S S M T W T F S S M T W T F S
      1 2 3 4 5 6 7 8 9 10 11 12 13 14 15 16 17 18 19 20 21 22 23 24 25 26 27 28 29 30
1700  E E D E E E E E E D E E E E E E D E E E E E E D E E E E E E
2300  E E E E E E E E E E E E E E E E E E E E E E E E E E E E E E

DEC   S M T W T F S S M T W T F S S M T W T F S S M T W T F S S M T
      1 2 3 4 5 6 7 8 9 10 11 12 13 14 15 16 17 18 19 20 21 22 23 24 25 26 27 28 29 30 31
1700  E D D E E E E E E D E E E E E E D E E E E E E E D E E E E
2300  E E E E E E E E E E E E E E E E E E E E E E E E E E
```

The company reserves the right to alter sailing times without prior notice.

FROM LONDON CONTINUED

▶ **NASSAU** CONTINUED

		Days	Depart	Arrive	Flight	Aircraft/Class	Stops	Airport	Arrive	Depart	Flight	Aircraft/Class
		--3----	1145Ⓝ	1615	BA265	747/FJM	0					
28 Oct–20 Dec		1--4-6-	1625④	2245	BA189	Concorde	2	MIA	1810	2200	UP255	73S/Y
3 Jan–30 Mar		1--4-6-	1625④	2245	BA189	Concorde	2	MIA	1810	2200	UP255	73S/Y

▶ **NEWCASTLE**

Days	Depart	Arrive	Flight	Aircraft/Class	Stops
12345--	0725①	0830	BA5942	B11§/M	0
Daily	0925①	1030	BA5944	320§/M	0
Daily	1245①	1350	BA5950	73S§/M	0
12345--	1500①	1605	BA5952	320/M	0
Daily	1630①	1735	BA5954	EQV/M	0
12345--	1800①	1905	BA5958	320§/M	0
Daily	2030①	2135	BA5960	757§/M	0

▶ **NEW ORLEANS**

Days	Depart	Arrive	Flight	Aircraft/Class	Stops	Airport	Arrive	Depart	Flight	Aircraft/Class
----567	1055④	1739	BA299	747/FJM	1	ORD	1335	1523	UA775	737§/FY
Daily	1355④	2129	BA297	747/FJM	1	ORD	1635	1908	UA519	73S/FY

▶ **NEWQUAY**

Days	Depart	Arrive	Flight	Aircraft/Class	Stops
------7	0915①	1020	BC813	DH7/Y	0
12345--	0915①	1055	BC803	DH7/Y	1
-----6-	1000①	1105	BC813	DH7/Y	0
12345--	1245①	1425	BC805	DH7/Y	1
12345--	1610①	1750	BC807	DH7/Y	1
------7	1945①	2050	BC819	DH7/Y	0
12345--	1945①	2110	BC809	DH7/Y	1

▶ **NEW YORK (JOHN F. KENNEDY)**

	Days	Depart	Arrive	Flight	Aircraft/Class	Stops
	Daily	1030④	0920	BA001	Concorde	0
	Daily	1100④	1350	BA175	747/FJM	0
	Daily	1200Ⓝ	1450	BA173	L10/FJM	0
	Daily	1415④	1705	BA177	747/FJM	0
	Daily	1830④	2120	BA179	747/FJM	0
28 Oct–17 Dec	Daily	1900④	1755	BA003	Concorde	0
3 Jan–30 Mar	12345-7	1900④	1755	BA003	Concorde	0

▶ **NEW YORK (NEWARK)**

Days	Depart	Arrive	Flight	Aircraft/Class	Stops
Daily	1030④	1320	BA185	747/FJM	0

▶ **NICE**

Days	Depart	Arrive	Flight	Aircraft/Class	Stops
Daily	0955②	1245	AF1831	AB3/CM	0
Daily	1230①	1520	BA342	757§/CM	0
Daily	1845①	2135	BA352	320/CM	0

▶ **OKLAHOMA CITY**

Days	Depart	Arrive	Flight	Aircraft/Class	Stops	Airport	Arrive	Depart	Flight	Aircraft/Class
Daily	0955Ⓝ	1610	BA229	D10/FJM	1	DFW	1415	1522	DL940	DC9/FM

▶ **OMAHA**

Days	Depart	Arrive	Flight	Aircraft/Class	Stops	Airport	Arrive	Depart	Flight	Aircraft/Class
----567	1055④	1658	BA299	747/FJM	1	ORD	1335	1537	UA617	727/FY
Daily	1355④	2038	BA297	747/FJM	1	ORD	1635	1905	UA395	727§/FY

▶ **OPORTO**

Days	Depart	Arrive	Flight	Aircraft/Class	Stops
Daily	0925①	1145	BA512	73S/CM	0
Daily	1755②	2005	TP483	727§/CY	0

Ⓝ Ⓢ Gatwick Terminals
Ⓐ Ⓑ Manchester Terminals
① ② ③ ④ Heathrow Terminals

The information printed opposite is taken from a 'British Airways Worldwide Timetable' and shows flights from London to (▶) various destinations. Days of the week are numbered as follows: Monday – 1, Tuesday – 2, etc. Where there is a transfer between aircraft, the details are given on the right hand side. The prefix BA denotes British Airways flight e.g., BA265.

15 On which days of the week does flight BA5952 *not* fly to Newcastle?

16 Reference flight BA003 to New York:

    a Which class of plane operates on this flight?
    b Calculate the flying time.
    c From which London airport does this flight depart?

17 A client who insists on travelling on British Airways needs to arrive in Nice sometime before 6 p.m. on 1 December.

    a Provide details of the flight number, the London Airport, the departure time using the 12 hour clock.
    b Calculate the flying time.

18 Find the time difference between flying to New York on 30 October by Concord using flight BA001 and flying on flight BA177.

19 How many daily flights are there from Gatwick to New York?

20 In flying to New Orleans on BA299, find the transfer time taken at Chicago airport (ORD).

21 A client required information regarding flying by British Airways to North Portugal on 3 November.

    a Give the time of departure and airport.
    b Calculate the flying time if Portugal was operating GMT on 3 November.

22 A passenger flies to Nassau via Miami (MIA) using flight BA189 on 3 December.

    a Calculate the actual flying time if the Bahamas are 5 hours behind GMT.
    b Will the passenger travel the whole journey on Concord?
    c On which days of the week does this flight operate.

26

Booking a holiday

France — Cote d'Azur

Property	Pool	Sleeping Capacity	LOW Sat.-Sat. (Mar 23,30 / Apr 6,13,20,27) 1 Week	Extra Week	ECONOMY Sat.-Sat. (May 4,11,18 / Sep 28 / Oct 5,12,19,26*) 1 Week	Extra Week	MID Sat.-Sat. (May 25 / June 1,8,15,22 / Aug 31 / Sep 7,14,21) 1 Week	Extra Week	HIGH Sat.-Sat. (June 29 / July 6,13,20,27 / Aug 3,10,17,24) 1 Week	Extra Week
3★										
QV 54 La Tartuca (p70) 2 week lets only	Shared pool	4/5	329	279	349	299	459	409	579	529
QA 81 Le Mas St. Jean (p75) 2 week lets only	Shared pool	4/6	369	319	379	329	489	439	709	659
QV 44 St Arnoux (p71)	Private pool	5	-	-	499	459	799	759	989	989
QV 111 Le Plateau (p71) 2 week lets only	Private pool	5	479	429	499	459	799	759	1099	1099
QV 94 Le Mas des Tilleuls (p68) 2 week lets only in High season	Private pool	5	-	-	-	-	579	559	759	739
QV 109 La Chesnaye (p84)	Private pool	6	479	429	499	459	799	769	999	999
QV 41 Villa Auriou (p71) 2 week lets only in High season	Private pool	6	479	429	499	459	849	789	1099	999
QV 114 Cameret (p78) 2 week lets only	Private pool	6	629	579	649	589	849	789	1249	1199
QV 117 Le Mas Baudisset (p84) Easter Supp: 30/3, 6/4 £220 per week	Private pool	6	879	819	899	839	1069	1009	1689	1629
QV 101 Villa Les Etoiles (p74) 2 week lets only		6	-	-	-	-	939	859	1309	1229
QV 23 Figanieres (p69) 2 week lets only	Private pool	6/7	-	-	559	499	879	819	1099	999
QV 15 La Clairiere (p73)	Private pool	6/8	529	509	569	549	959	939	1199	1199
QV 107 La Roseraie (p84)	Private pool	8	479	449	499	469	859	839	1099	1099
QV 90 Villa Billon (p76)	Private pool	8/10	-	-	-	-	869	849	1099	1099
4★										
QA 96 Parc Bellevue (p74)	Shared pool	4	389	369	399	379	499	489	599	589
QA 08/42 Les Bois D'Amont (p67)	Shared pool	2/4	529	479	569	529	609	569	709	669
QV 72 Les Essares (p75) 2 week lets only	Private pool	4/6	-	-	-	-	949	879	1459	1379
QV 87 La Louisane (p72)	Private pool	5	519	509	539	529	1029	1019	1459	1429
QV 53 Villa Sufit (p70) 2 week lets only	Private pool	6	-	-	-	-	1059	999	1519	1459
QV 92 Les Romarins (p76) 2 week lets only in High season	Private pool	6	529	519	559	539	979	959	1449	1479
QV 99 Les Oliviers (p76) Easter Supp: 30/3,6/4 £220 per week	Private pool	6	899	839	939	869	1249	1179	1939	1879
QV 67 Villa Sennette (p73) Easter only 23/3,30/3 & High season: fortnightly lets only	Private pool	6/8	1169	1109	-	-	1239	1179	1929	1869
QV 91 Villa Espourounes (p75) 2 week lets only	Private pool	7	-	-	-	-	-	-	1929	1869
QV 58 Saint Laurent (p70)	Private pool	7/8	-	-	-	-	999	969	1359	1309
QA 76 Vaugrenier (p75) 2 week lets only		8	569	559	599	579	769	759	1159	1139
QV 103 Le Mas Des Pins (p74) 2 week lets only in High season	Shared pool	8	1109	969	1139	1019	1389	1269	1829	1709
QV 10 Peyrebelle (p66)	Private pool	8	489	469	529	499	909	889	1249	1229
QV 105 Les Cypres (p74)	Private pool	8	489	469	519	499	909	889	1249	1229
QV 112 Villa Normand (p71) 2 week lets only	Private pool	8	629	559	639	569	1089	989	1709	1629
QV 60 Ribes Rocque (p68) 2 week lets only	Private pool	8	679	659	1149	1129	1509	1489	2139	2119
QV 33 Les Tableaux (p77) 2 week lets only	Private pool	10/12	779	709	859	779	1909	1839	2329	2259
5★										
QV 85 La Fenice (p78)	Private pool	6	659	639	709	689	1459	1439	1789	1769
QV 96 Villa Quera (p72)	Private pool	6	-	-	-	-	1629	1559	2199	2129
QV 32 La Cousteline (p67) Easter Supp per week: 23/3,30/3,6/4 £220. 31/8 £940	Private pool	6/8	1119	1039	1339	1249	1659	1569	2599	2509
QV 69 La Renaude (p67) 2 week lets only	Private pool	7	889	789	959	849	1469	1449	2329	2219
QV 97 Le Mas des Valerianes (p76) 2 week lets only in High season	Private pool	7/8	-	-	-	-	1469	1449	2379	2369
QV 102 Le Mas des Violettes (p72) 2 week lets only in High season	Private pool	7/9	-	-	1049	969	1549	1459	2389	2369
QV 73 La Grande Bastide (p76) Withdrawn		10	-	-	-	-	-	-	-	-

Price Per Property Per Half Month

Property	Pool	Sleeping Capacity	Apr 1-15	Apr 16-30	May 1-15	May 16-31	Jun 1-15	Jun 16-30	Jul 1-15	Jul 16-31	Aug 1-15	Aug 16-31	Sep 1-15	Sep 16-30	Oct 1-15	Oct 16-31
3★																
QV 04 Mas D'Emponse 2 (p73)	Private pool	4	-	-	-	-	-	-	2159	2249	2249	2159	1349	1129	809	729
QA 03 Le Degustaou 2 (p69)	Shared pool	6	-	-	629	629	749	749	1139	1139	1139	1139	749	749	-	-
QV 01 Les Faisses (p68)	Private pool	9/10	-	-	1129	1129	1579	1579	2159	2559	2559	2559	1889	1579	-	-
4★																
QA 02 Le Degustaou 1 (p69)	Private pool	5	-	-	699	699	919	919	1309	1309	1309	1309	919	919	-	-
QV 113 Entrechaux (p78)	Private pool	6	-	-	-	-	-	-	3579	3879	3879	3579	-	-	-	-
QV 110 Moulin de Pierrefeu †	Private pool	6	959	959	1269	-	-	-	3659	3659	3659	3659	-	-	-	-
QV 56 Bramepan (p69)	Private pool	7/8	-	-	-	-	-	-	2059	2509	2749	2619	-	-	-	-
QV 88 Le Mas Ste Anne (p70)	Private pool	8/10	-	-	-	-	-	3498	4548	4548	4788	4788	-	-	-	-
QV 46 Peymenade (p68) Withdrawn																
5★																
QV 36 Cateric (p66)	Private pool	7	-	-	-	-	-	-	4229	4229	4889	4889	-	-	-	-
QV 05 Mas d'Emponse I (p73)	Private pool	8	-	-	1559	1859	2179	2309	4569	4779	4779	4569	2309	2179	1419	1219
QV 74 Pijaubert (p66)	Private pool	12	-	-	-	-	-	-	4429	4949	4949	4949	-	-	-	-
QV 06 L'Abri-Cotier (p77)	Private pool	9	-	-	1889	2169	-	-	6939	7139	7139	6939	-	2999	1539	1309

What the price includes: see page 4
Refundable breakages/cleaning deposit payable to owner or his agent locally on arrival.
Cot Hire: £20 per week.
No child discount.

Insurance: Cancellation, curtailment and delay insurance are included. You are strongly advised to add the optional holiday and motor insurances (see page 16).
† Price includes heated pool, linen & daily maid service.
* one week only.

Optional flight or ferry crossing: Please request. Please note that if we neither book a ferry crossing nor air flights there will be a supplement of £20 per booking.
Optional car hire: see page 2.
Heating (when available) paid locally.

The details shown opposite are taken from the villa holiday price guide to 'France and Italy *MEON* Style'. It is a typically informative guide showing the area of France, the name of the villa, sleeping numbers and prices at different times of the year. Before you attempt to answer the questions, read the conditions at the bottom of the page.

1 Mr & Mrs Castle and their 2 friends require a holiday on the Cote d'Azur during the week commencing 7 April. They wish to stay in a 4 star apartment close to Grasse. The travel agent suggests Les Bois D'Amont and confirms its availability. Mr Castle and friends will make their own travel arrangements. What is the price per person?

2 A group of 4 adults and 4 children wish to book a week's holiday commencing 7 July. They require a swimming pool but do not mind if it is shared. Cost is very important and they are looking for the lowest possible price.

The travel agency is requested to book a return ferry crossing through Meon for 2 cars and occupants at the following single rates:

   Car – £85, Adult fare – £13.50, Child fare – £8.00.

   a If Saint Laurent is already booked suggest the best alternative.
   b Calculate the price per person for the accommodation (to nearest £).
   c What is the total invoice charge as presented by the travel agent?

3 The Smith family (2 adults, 2 children) and the Howard family (2 adults and a baby), wish to book the Villa du Lac for the 3 weeks commencing either 12 May or 19 May. Find the total difference in price between the two periods.

4 A party of six wished to book a fortnight's holiday anytime in July. They stipulate they require a private pool and put a limit on cost of £300 per person which they subsequently agree to raise by £10 per person. Meon would be expected to book air travel but this would not affect the cost limit for the villa. Suggest the best possible property to fit in with their requirements.

5 Give the total cost per person for a holiday taken in the Villa Maeva by 7 adults during the period 11 August to 25 August. The cost of the air travel (arranged privately) was £130 per person and the hire cost of a mini bus was £480 per week (Answer to the nearest £).

6 Eight friends booked La Cousteline for the 2 weeks commencing 14 April. Find the cost per person if they make their own travel arrangements (to the nearest £).

7 Mr & Mrs Felton and their 2 children require a villa with private pool for the 2 weeks commencing 7 July. Their travel agent is asked to find the cheapest possible property for that period. Which property would you suggest?

The details opposite are taken from the Silk Cut Faraway Holidays brochure and form the basis for the following:

8 Calculate the total cost for a couple staying half board at Dian Bay in the Ocean View Suite for 7 nights from 1 January.

9 Prepare a quotation for Jane Wilson who is interested in a holiday in Antigua. She will require 9 nights at a hotel able to provide full board from 18 April. She prefers to travel Club World.

10 Mr & Mrs Dobbs make enquiries about taking their 10-year-old daughter to the Halcyon Cove for 12 nights from 18 July.

    a What quotation should be given to the Dobbs family (assume the single rate will not apply)?

    b The Dobbs family later decided to book into the Lord Nelson and take half board. Find the amount of money Mr Dobbs paid for the holiday.

11 Susan and Philip are planning their honeymoon to follow their wedding on 29 September. They ask a travel agency to arrange 7 nights half board at the Halcyon Cove in the Garden Superior twin room. They wish to travel Club World. Calculate the cost of the honeymoon from the information supplied.

Departures on or between	1 Nov 7 Dec 90		8 Dec 31 Dec 90		1 Jan 25 Jan 91		26 Jan 10 Apr 91		11 Apr 30 Jun 91		1 Jul 15 Sep 91		16 Sep 30 Nov 91		8 Dec 10 Apr 91	11 Apr 30 Nov 91
Hotel	Meal Basis	Hol. No.	7 Night	Extra Night	7 Night	Extra Night	7 Night	Extra Night	7 Night	Extra Night	7 Night	Extra Night	7 Night	Extra Night	7 Night	Extra Night	Per Night	Per Night
Lord Nelson	–	ANLN01	617	23	987	33	719	32	737	33	656	23	756	23	666	23	17	17
Dian Bay	–	ANDB02	750	45	1160	61	890	59	910	60	791	45	891	45	791	45	41	25
Halcyon Cove	–	ANHC03	680	30	1231	67	860	57	875	59	683	33	778	33	698	33	61	–
Galley Bay	FB	ANGB04	918	62	1430	93	971	74	1119	96	957	62	1036	62	957	62	42	34
PRICES INCLUDE PRIVATE TRANSFERS																	

HOTEL SUPPLEMENTS (Per person per night)
Lord Nelson – Half Board £26
Dian Bay – One Bedroom Ocean View Suite £4, Half Board £27
Halcyon Cove – Garden Superior Twin £8, Poolside Deluxe Twin £16, Ocean Front Deluxe £24, Half Board £27
Galley Bay – Beachfront Twin £14 (£9.00 6 Apr – 30 Nov)

FLIGHT INFORMATION

Flight Supplements:
British Airways – Club World £498 (1 Jul – 31 Aug), £595 (1 Apr – 30 Jun and 1 Sep – 30 Nov), £650 (1 – 31 Dec), £855 (1 Jan – 31 May)

Flight Information:
British Airways – Flights for Gatwick Tuesday, Wednesday, Saturday and Sunday, departing in the morning. Return landing next day in the morning

— 27 —

Deposits and cancellations

Hotels, tour operators, cruise organisers will all require a deposit when a booking is made. That is, a sum of money is requested as a show of good faith that the booking will be taken up. Different organisations have differing rates and conditions relating to deposits but here is a typical example:

A tour operator advertised a holiday for £300 per week and requested a deposit of £65 at the time of booking. If the holiday was subsequently cancelled by the client the following terms applied:

Period of cancellation	Amount to be paid
Up to 6 weeks before holiday	The deposit
42 days–29 days before holiday	50% of holiday cost
28 days–22 days ,, ,,	60% ,, ,, ,,
21 days– 4 days ,, ,,	75% ,, ,, ,,
Under 4 days ,, ,,	100% ,, ,, ,,

1 If a holiday was cancelled 7 weeks before the holiday commenced, how much money was retained by the tour operator?

2 A holiday was cancelled 25 days before commencement. How much money was paid in total by the client?

3 Mr & Mrs Belton had booked a week's holiday due to start on 17 July. Unfortunately, the holiday had to be cancelled on 28 June. How much money did the Belton's lose?

An insurance against cancellation can usually be taken out for a fee at the time of booking a holiday. This will reimburse any costs for which a holidaymaker may be responsible providing there is a genuine reason, e.g., illness, redundancy. Of course, the insurance/cancellation fee cannot be reclaimed.

4 A client paid a deposit of £65 and a cancellation fee of £15 for a holiday. Later, because of illness, the holiday had to be cancelled. What was the final amount paid by the client?

5 Use the terms at the beginning of this chapter to work out this question:

Two friends booked the £300 holiday to commence on 2 September. Stephen decided to pay a £15 cancellation fee but Paul did not. On 31 August, Stephen broke his leg and could not continue with the holiday arrangements and Paul would not go away on his own. How much money did the cancelled holiday cost

a Stephen?
b Paul?

— 28 —

Value Added Tax (VAT)

VAT is a customer tax, that is, the cost of paying for this tax is added to the customer's bill. As is the case with all taxes, it is a means of raising money (revenue) to enable the government to pay for the provision of benefits and services. The tax is paid to the Customs & Excise. The rate is set as a percentage of the value of certain goods and services but it can be changed by the government. Other members of the European Community (EC) have different rates. Businesses are registered for VAT purpose so that they can charge for and reclaim this tax. Look out for the VAT registration number on an invoice.

In this chapter use a VAT rate of 17.5% unless otherwise stated.

Example

A restaurant charged £12.00 plus VAT for an evening meal. Calculate the total price paid by the customer.

Method

      Money required by the restaurant £12.00
      17.5% VAT   £2.10

      Price paid by the customer   £14.10

      NB   The VAT (£2.10) is sent to the
              Customs & Excise.

It isn't always as straightforward as this. Certain services are exempt from VAT and others are zero rated. At the present time transport is zero rated but this could change to come into line with other EEC countries.

VAT must be paid on the 'mark up' by a travel agent etc.

Example

A travel agent arranges a holiday costing £500 to which he adds a mark up of 10%. Calculate the VAT that must be paid on this mark up.

Method

      Basic Cost   £500.00
      10% Mark up   £50.00
      17.5% of £50 =   £8.75 VAT.

1   A hotel needs to charge £20 per head for an evening meal with drinks in order to make a reasonable profit. If VAT at 17.5% must be added to this charge, what is the total bill for a party of 6 diners?

2   The cost of a holiday to a travel agent was £550 and to this he intended adding a mark up of 12%. Calculate the VAT levied on this mark up.

3   As a businessman, the owner of a hotel can claim back the £2500 VAT he paid when making purchases from his suppliers (for wine etc.) but he must pay £8050 VAT he has added to the bills of his customers. What is the amount of VAT the hotelier should send to the Customs & Excise?

4   A travel agency sells a holiday package for £1200 and earns commission of 10% on this sale from the tour operator. To enable the agency to earn the full commission, the operator also pays the VAT of 17.5% on the commission.

    a   Calculate the VAT paid by the operator to the agency.
    b   What was the total amount paid by the operator to the agency?
    c   Why should the operator pay this VAT? (For discussion.)

5   A travel agency earns a commission of £60.00 from a car hire company.

    a   If VAT is at 20% find the total amount the agency receives from the car hire company.

    b   How much of this money will the agency eventually send to Customs & Excise?

– 29 –

Hiring a car

Travel agencies are able to arrange car hire in almost every country in the world. To encourage and reward the travel agents for providing this service they are paid a percentage commission by the car hire companies.

The information opposite is taken from the 'Avis Supervalue Europe' brochure and gives prices depending on the type of car and length of rental. You will see that opposite to the name of the country are the dates during which the rates apply. The class of car (Mini, economy, medium) is denoted by a group letter (A, B, C) followed by an example of a car type in each category. The rate code (EE, E1, E2) refers to the length of rental (7–13 days, 14–20 days, 21+ days). Prices shown are per day. These details are used in the documentation sent by the Travel Agent to the hire company.

Example

Calculate the cost of hiring a Group B car in Greece for 10 days in August.

Method

The cost of hiring a Group B car in Greece during August is £36 per day.

Therefore for 10 days the cost = 10 × £36 = £360

1   Find the cost of hiring a Group A car for 22 days in Ireland during May.

2   A family will be holidaying in Holland during October and wish to rent a Group B car for 17 days.

    Calculate:

    a   The cost of the car hire

    b   The commission earned by the travel agent if the rate was (i) 5% (ii) 8%

Greece

			01 Apr '90-30 Jun '90		
			01 Oct '90-31 Mar '91		
Rate Name/SuperValue		Rate Code	EE	E2	E3
Class	Group	Example of car	7-13 DAYS	14-20 DAYS	21+ DAYS
Mini	A	Subaru M.70DL	£28	£27	£25
Mini	B	Nissan Cherry 1.0	£30	£29	£27
Economy	C	Nissan Sunny 1.3	£34	£32	£31

Greece

			01 Jul '90-30 Sep '90		
Rate Name/SuperValue		Rate Code	EE	E2	E3
Class	Group	Example of car	7-13 DAYS	14-20 DAYS	21+ DAYS
Mini	A	Subaru M.70DL	£34	£32	£31
Mini	B	Nissan Cherry 1.0	£36	£34	£32
Economy	C	Nissan Sunny 1.3	£40	£38	£36

Holland

			01 Apr '90-31 Mar '91		
Rate Name/SuperValue		Rate Code	EE	E2	E3
Class	Group	Example of car	7-13 DAYS	14-20 DAYS	21+ DAYS
Mini	A	Citroen AX 11RE	£27	£24	£22
Mini	B	Opel Corsa 1.2LS	£31	£28	£25
Economy	C	Opel Kadett 1.3	£35	£32	£28

Ireland

			01 Apr '90-30 Jun '90, 16 Sep '90-14 Dec '90		
			01 Jan '91-31 Mar '91		
Rate Name/SuperValue		Rate Code	EE	E2	E3
Class	Group	Example of car	7-13 DAYS	14-20 DAYS	21+ DAYS
Mini	A	Opel Corsa 1.0	£33	£30	£26
Economy	B	Opel Kadett 1.2	£39	£35	£31
Medium	C	Toyota Carina 1.6	£49	£44	£39

Ireland

			01 Jul '90-15 Sep '90		
			15 Dec '90-31 Dec '90		
Rate Name/SuperValue		Rate Code	EE	E2	E3
Class	Group	Example of car	7-13 DAYS	14-20 DAYS	21+ DAYS
Mini	A	Opel Corsa 1.0	£41	£37	£33
Economy	B	Opel Kadett 1.2	£46	£41	£37
Medium	C	Toyota Carina 1.6	£56	£50	£45

Israel

			01 Apr '90-30 Apr '90, 01 Jul '90-31 Aug '90		
			15 Dec '90-10 Jan '91		
Rate Name/SuperValue		Rate Code	EE	E2	E3
Class	Group	Example of car	7-13 DAYS	14-20 DAYS	21+ DAYS
Mini	A	Autobianchi Y10	£41	£37	£33
Mini	B	Peugeot 205 (AC)	£46	£41	£37
Economy	C	Fiat Tipo (AC)	£55	£50	£44

3   Mr & Mrs Granger will be spending the month of September in Greece. They ask their travel agent to quote for the cheapest possible hire car from 10 September to 23 September inclusive. Provide a quotation from the available information.

4   Five friends will be holidaying in Ireland and need to hire a car for the period 4 August to 20 August inclusive.

   a   Suggest a Group of car and give the price.
   b   What rate code should be entered by the travel agent on any documentation.

5   Four friends need to rent a car for 21 days during a visit to Israel in April. They decide a Group B car would be satisfactory.

Calculate:

   a   the cost per person
   b   the commission earned by the travel agent for arranging the hire car if the rate was 5%.
   c   the total amount paid by the rental company to the travel agent if the VAT on the commission was also paid to the Agent. (Assume the rate of VAT was 17.5%.)

− 30 −

Chartering

When a tour operator compiles a holiday involving air travel, there are two methods of costing to consider. A journey can be made by the normal 'Scheduled' air flight, which is similar to using a regular train or bus service. Alternatively, a plane can be hired or 'chartered' just as a college may hire a coach to transport a group of students on a visit. Chartering is usually cheaper but with aircraft it can have its drawbacks. At peak (holiday) times, scheduled air traffic gets preference over chartered flights when being allocated air space and that can cause delay and frustration among passengers and ultimately cause problems for travel agents (for discussion).

Let's charter a plane

A 130 seater aircraft can be chartered to Spain for £12 600 per return trip on 25 consecutive Fridays. Let us assume that on average the aircraft will be 90% full (load factor = 90%). On the first return leg the aircraft will be empty and the same is true on the last outward leg.

Therefore the number of passengers carried will be

$$24 \times 130 \times \frac{90}{100} = 2808$$

(24 *passenger* return flights, 130 seats, 90% full)
The cost of the aircraft is:
£12 600 × 25 (aircraft cost × number of return trips) = £315 000

$$\text{Therefore the cost per passenger} = \frac{315\ 000}{2808} = £112.18$$

1   A 99 seater BAC One–Eleven can be chartered to Malaga for £11 000 per return trip on 21 consecutive Sundays during the holiday season. The tour operator estimated an 80% load factor. Calculate the cost per passenger return trip (to the nearest £).

2   A Boeing Super 737 can be chartered for £15 000 per return trip and is capable of seating 106 passengers. Calculate the cost per passenger if the plane was chartered for 16 weekly flights and a load factor of 90% was expected.

3   A 180 seater Boeing 757 can be chartered to fly to Athens on 20 consecutive Saturdays for £21 000 per return flight. Find the return cost per passenger, assuming a loading factor of 80% and a total of £10 per person airport taxes.

4   A 54 seater coach is hired to transport holidaymakers at £510 per return journey on 11 consecutive Saturdays. If a 75% loading factor is envisaged, calculate the cost per passenger return trip (to the nearest £).

5   A group of 106 businessmen needed to attend a conference in Rome. They asked a travel agent to find the cost of chartering a plane. The agent found the cost to be £12 000. Find the cost per person (to the nearest £).

– 31 –

Graphs

Graphs can be used to display information in a simple easy-to-read form. Comparing data from lists of figures can be time consuming and may lead to inaccuracies. A graph displayed on a wall can be a semi-permanent reminder of the state of business e.g. occupancy, profit, turnover, costs. Computers can now be programmed to present facts and figures in graphical form.

Study the line graph below.

The horizontal axis A–B refers to the months of trading.
The vertical axis A–C refers to the turnover (in £s) during the year.

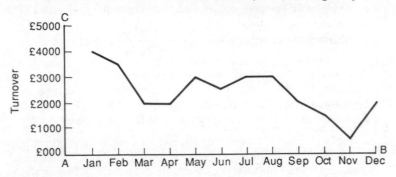

To determine the turnover in March, first find March on the horizontal axis and then find the plot vertically above. Read the £20 000 in the left hand column level with the plot.

Use the graph above to answer the following questions.

1   What was the turnover in July?

2   What was the worst month in terms of business carried out?

3   What was the difference in turnover between the best and worst months?

More than one piece of information can be shown on the same graph. The following graph shows two sets of facts. The continuous line shows the total income for each week but the broken line shows the total costs. From these details we can quickly determine the profit or loss.

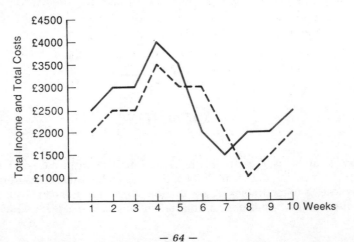

The total income in week 1 was £2500 and the total costs were £2000, therefore the net profit was £500.

Notice how easy it is to check at a glance whether the business is in a profit or loss situation.

4 In week 3
   a What was the total income?
   b What were the total costs?
   c What was the net profit?

5 What was the net situation in week 7?

6 What was the profit in week 9?

7 Which week showed the highest profit?

8 Which was the worst week?

Here is an example of a block graph. This graph shows the number of people frequenting the badminton courts during a week.

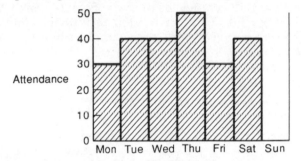

9 How many people attended on Wednesday?

10 What was the lowest attendance (excluding Sunday)?

11 On what day were the courts closed?

12 Assuming we wished to show an all round improvement during a second week, how could we depict two sets of figures on a block graph? (For discussion.)

13 Draw a line graph to show the percentage occupancy of an hotel using the following information. Let the horizontal axis represent the weeks and the vertical axis represent the occupancy.

Week 1	Week 2	Week 3	Week 4	Week 5	Week 6
25%	40%	35%	70%	70%	60%

14 Draw a block graph to show the number of individual holidays sold during a four week period.

Week 1	Week 2	Week 3	Week 4
200	350	100	50

15 Draw a line graph to show the domestic and overseas holiday sales during a six month period. (Use two different colours, or pen and pencil.)

Month	Jan	Feb	Mar	Apr	May	Jun
UK Holidays	£2000	£2000	£3000	£1000	£4000	£5000
Overseas Holidays	£10000	£11000	£8000	£5000	£4000	£4000

– 32 –

Pie charts

A good method of illustrating the division of costs, income, holidays etc., is by using a 'Pie Chart'. A circle (or pie) is divided into segments showing the proportion of 'parts' to the 'whole'. Study the following diagrams.

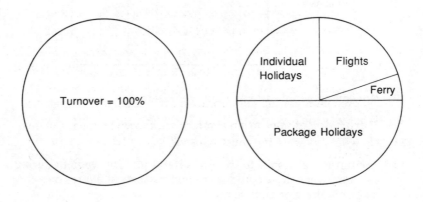

The circle (360°) represents the turnover of a travel agency. The diagram on the right shows how the turnover is made up by dividing 360° into proportional parts. Package holidays account for 50% of business and is represented by 180° (50% of 360). Ferry bookings account for 5% (18°) of business. Flight bookings account for 20% (72°) of business. Individual holidays account for 25% (90°) of business. Together they must add up to 360°. The chart can be made easier to read by differently colouring each segment.

1 The chart shows how the 720 staff of an organisation is divided.

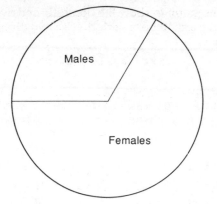

Measure the arc of each segment to find the value of each part of the total labour force.

NB First divide the 720 staff by 360 to find the number of employees represented by 1°, then multiply by the number of degrees in the arc.

2 The owner of a coach company wanted to depict the direct costs in the form of a pie chart. Produce a chart to show the following information. (First find the total costs.)

Depreciation of vehicles – £40 000, Fuel costs – £180 000, Insurance – £30 000, Labour £110 000.

3 A tourist office showed information provided for the public in the form of a pie chart. Give the segment size of each of the following:

Places of interest 20%, Entertainment 15%, Tours 10%, Accommodation 10%, In-town directions 40%, Others 5%.

4 The division of sales in a restaurant are shown by means of this pie chart. Find the value of each part if the total sales were £180 000.

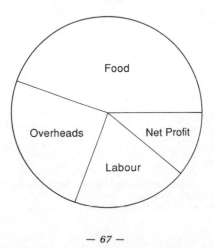

— 33 —

Mixed tests

In working through these tests use the information given in the previous chapters except where details are provided.

Test 1

1 13 hours 40 minutes + 2 hours 32 minutes + 53 minutes.

2 Mary worked a 37 hour week for which she was paid £3.06 per hour plus time and a half for overtime. Calculate her gross wages in a week when she worked 42 hours.

3 A travel agent priced a holiday as follows: Travelling £115.50, Accommodation £472.80, Insurance £17.16. Find the total charge made to the client.

4 An agent sold a holiday to the value of £2250. If his commission on these sales was 10%, how much did he earn?

5 It was decided to charge senior citizens 80% of the normal admission price of 90p to use the swimming pool. What would a couple pay together for one visit if the husband qualified for this reduction but his wife did not?

6 Share the cost of the £586 hire charge for a mini-bus between 8 students.

7 Express 42 km to the nearest mile.

8 A coach averaged 38 miles per hour over 4.5 hours. What distance was covered?

9 If 1 kg is approximately 2.2. lbs

    a How many lbs approximately are there in 12 kg?
    b Express 33 lbs in kg.

10 A travel operator cut the price of a holiday from £320 to £272. Calculate the percentage reduction.

Test 2

1 Express the following in terms of the 24 hour clock.

    a 5 minutes past midnight.
    b A quarter past eight in the evening.
    c 10.20 p.m.
    d 7.45 a.m.

2 If £1 = 9.6 French francs, calculate how many francs a tourist would receive for £1000.

3 The distance between two towns on a map was 13.5 cm. What is the true distance between these towns if the scale of the map was 2 cm = 5 km.

4 1.647 ÷ 0.6

5 A car driver reckoned to get 34 mpg out of his car on a long journey. How many gallons of fuel would be used in travelling 731 miles?

6 Tom, Paul, John and Dave arranged a two weeks holiday, cruising on the Norfolk Broads. They would commence their holiday on 30 June and for that period the cost of boat hire was £447 per week. Other costs were: Cancellation fee £14 per week, Car parking £5 per week, Television £15 per week, Fuel £36 in total.

On booking Tom sent a cheque to cover an initial fee of £55 per week and the cancellation fee of £14 per week. Calculate how much remains to be paid at the time of the holiday

a by Tom
b by the others.

7 The Hotel Exclusive required a 5% deposit for all bookings. What deposit should be sent to the Hotel to confirm a 'phone reservation' involving £655 for accommodation?

8 Mr & Mrs Hill received a phone call on 22 October at 8 a.m. from their daughter in Tokyo. What time was it in Japan?

9

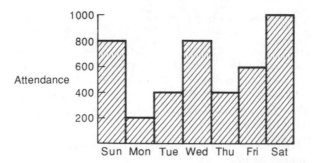

The graph shows the average number of people attending a Sea Experience Centre during June, July and August. The centre employs mainly part time staff.

a On which day should the centre employ the least staff?
b On which 3 days should the centre be fully staffed?
c What was the average weekly takings if children accounted for two thirds of the visitors and the prices of admission were: Adults £2, Children £1?

10 Of the 20 000 holidays arranged by a tour operator, 17 500 were for visits overseas. What percentage of the total was for holidays in the UK?

Test 3

1 A holiday was costed by a travel agent at £750. To this she added a mark up of 15% of costs. What price would the agent charge for this holiday?

2 A client wished to arrive in Cherbourg early afternoon on 17 May. Using the P & O table (page 51) advise the client of the ferry's sailing time from Portsmouth and also say what time the ferry would be expected to arrive in Cherbourg (local time).

3 On average 45% of the users of sports facilities at the Bampton Leisure Centre were women. A count on a particular evening showed there were 135 women present. On statistics available state how many people were estimated to be using the facilities altogether.

4 If the statistics used in Question 3 were displayed in the form of a pie chart, how many degrees would represent the men?

5 Cancel

$$\textbf{a} \quad \frac{36}{81} \qquad \textbf{b} \quad \frac{100}{105} \qquad \textbf{c} \quad \frac{4}{64}$$

6 A driver has the option of travelling to his holiday destination by two routes. Route A involved 270 miles using motorways and averaging 45 mph. Route B involved 234 miles of non-motorway and averaging 36 mph. Which route is the quickest and by how much if the driver stops for a break of 30 minutes after every 2 hours of driving?

7 The currency rate displayed inside a bank showed the following exchange rate for £1 sterling.

USA $ We buy at 1.90 We sell at 1.78

How many £s would a tourist receive for $100?

8 The price for a holiday in Italy was £425 per person, per week. A group reduction rate was advertised as follows:

'One free place in every group of ten.'

a Calculate the total charge made for a party of 16 tourists.
b If the group shared this cost, how much would each pay (to the nearest penny)?
c If the party persuaded 4 more people to join them, what would be the new shared cost per person?

9 A plan of a holiday chalet (shown below) is drawn to a scale of 1:200

a What is (i) the length in metres?
        (ii) the width in metres?
b What length would represent a 2 metre bed?

10 A cruise departed Southampton on 18 January 1991 and returned on 14 March 1991. How many days (inclusive) did the cruise last?

Test 4

1 a 100 × £4.27   **b** £1494 ÷ 100

2 A courier escorted a group of 36 senior citizens on a trip to York in a 54 seater coach. The coach was due to leave York at 18.30 and the passengers were told to be back ready to leave 10 minutes earlier.

At 18.25 the courier counted a total of 21 empty seats:

a What time would the courier have told the passengers to be back on the coach? Think carefully.
b How many passengers were missing at 18.25?

3 A travel consultant earned a commission of 9% on overseas flights and 7% on domestic flights. Calculate the total commission earned on £28 000 of overseas business and £5300 of business representing flights within the UK.

4 A travel agent had purchased his business for £500 000. After one year's trading he had made a profit of £30 000. Find the percentage return on his outlay.

5 At 12.05 on 24 April an aircraft departed Gatwick and arrived Athens 17.45 (local time). Find the actual flying time.

6 A tour operator costed a package holiday at £279. If the operator worked on a net profit of 10% on the selling price, calculate the price that should be advertised for this holiday.

7 What price should be quoted by a travel agent for a family of 2 adults and 3 children (ages 5, 7 and baby) who wish to travel on the 13.00 sailing from Portsmouth to Cherbourg on 20 August and return on the 17.00 sailing on 1 September?

8 A car driver sets out from Leicester at 7 a.m. and arrives Aberystwyth at 12.15 p.m., having taken a break of three quarters of an hour on the way. The driver noted the cars speedo reading was 017294 when he started the journey and 017456 when he arrived at his destination.

a Calculate the average travelling mph attained during the journey.
b If the car commenced the journey with a full tank of petrol and required 5.4 gallons to refill the tank at Aberystwyth, what mpg did the car achieve?

9 A coach hire company offers a 22 seater coach of £190 and a 51 seater coach at £400 for a certain journey. Calculate the cost of the most economical combination of coaches to transport 284 passengers.

10 A lady requested information regarding a ski resort, particularly its height above sea level. The travel clerk found the height was 1450 metres but the lady wanted that expressed in feet. If 1 metre is approximately 3.3 feet, what is the height the client should be given?

Test 5

1 a Find the area of carpet required in a hotel bedroom measuring 3.2 m × 3.75 m.
b Calculate the cost of the carpet @ £7.25 per square metre.

2 John delayed exchanging 3000 German marks for one day. The rate increased from DM2.93 to DM3 to the £. State whether John gained or lost and by how much (to the nearest £).

3 Calculate the total return cost of Gill and Paul White taking their caravan to France using the 09.00 Portsmouth/Cherbourg crossing on 20 July and returning 08.00 on 15 August. The length of the car and caravan are 4.42 m and 5.35 m respectively. The White's wish to travel Executive Club Class.

4 The Whites (Question 3) met another couple on the return crossing who are shareholders in P & O European Ferries and who therefore qualify for a discount of 40% off their fares for cars and occupants but not caravans or extras such as Club Class,

cabins etc. If the Whites had been shareholders how much money would they have saved on their return fares?

5   It is 11 a.m. New Year's Day in New Zealand. What is the time and date on the Eastern coast of the USA?

6   £340.4 ÷ 5

7   A courier accompanying a coach tour through the Rhine Gorge offered to arrange a cruise down the Rhine for 25 of the party. They were to embark on the hydrofoil at Cologne at 08.45. The coach would meet the boat at Mainz at 12.55. The cost of the trip was DM195 per person but there was a discount of 20% for groups of 15 or more. Find:

a   The length of the cruise in hours and minutes.
b   The total amount in pounds sterling collected by the courier to pay for the cruise if £1 = 2.93 marks (to the nearest £).

8   An hotel chef costs a meal at £5.60. If his manager has instructed him to make a gross profit of 65% on the selling price, what should he set as the selling price of the meal?

9   A Boeing 757 shuttle left Manchester with 35 of its 195 seats unoccupied. What was the percentage occupancy of the aircraft?

10   A travel agent advised a client to be certain to take insurance cover from home to home. If the client was leaving home on 28 June and returning on 1 August how many days should be covered?

Test 6

1   Mrs Elder was about to visit her son in Australia and she had been informed by her travel adviser that her luggage must not exceed 23 kg. The only scales she possessed showed the weight of her luggage to be 49 lbs. Is Mrs Elder's luggage within the prescribed limit? (She assumed 1 kg = 2.2 lbs.)

2   A motorist set out from Ostend to drive the 650 miles to Salzburg. He used his car clock which remained set at UK time throughout the journey. He left Ostend at 9.30 a.m. and arrived in Luxemburg at 3.48 p.m. The second day he left Luxemburg at 8.45 a.m. and arrived at Stuttgart at 2 p.m. On the final day he left Stuttgart at 9.15 a.m. arriving at his destination at 3.12 p.m. If he stopped each day for a 1 hour lunch break, what was his average mph for the whole journey?

3   Express the distance between Ostend and Salzburg (Question 2) to the nearest km.

4 Assuming the rate of VAT is 17.5% and an agent received a commission of £150 for arranging car hire, calculate the total amount received by the agent from the car hire company.

5 Design and draw a graph showing the following 2 sets of information:

Visitors to car museum

UK	150	200	125	75	150	250	225
Overseas	50	75	125	100	75	75	50

Days of the Week

Mon	Tue	Wed	Thu	Fri	Sat	Sun

6 The statistical returns of a restaurant for one week were as follows:

Sales – £4000, Food and Drink cost – £1600, Labour costs – £1000, Overheads – £1000.

Calculate the gross profit as a percentage of sales.

7 A traveller departed Gatwick 11.00 on Saturday 3 August and arrived Auckland 06.15 (local time) two days later. If an 8.5 hour transfer was made at Los Angeles, calculate the actual flying time.

8 A coach company planned a trip from Glasgow to Blackpool to view the illuminations. If the coach averages 10 mpg and the distance between the towns is 190 miles, what is the expected fuel cost if the fuel price is £2.35 per gallon.

9 Tickets sold for a performance at the Phoenix Theatre were as follows:

34 @ £9,   125 @ £7.25,   118 @ £5.50

Only 40% of the most expensive seats were taken but all other seats were fully sold. Calculate the maximum *possible* takings.

10 An hotel had 20 double bedrooms at £31.50 per person and 30 single bedrooms at £36.75 per person. 13 double bedrooms and 18 single bedrooms were fully occupied.

   a Find the percentage occupancy of:
     (i)   The double bedrooms
     (ii) The single bedrooms
     (iii) The hotel as a whole
   b If the total sales for the 24 hours were £2700, calculate the receipts from the apartments as a % of sales.

Test 7

1 The organiser of a day trip for 210 senior citizens to the coast had a quote from a coach company as follows:

25 seater – £240, 56 seater – £490

a Find (i) the best (cheapest) combination of coaches the organiser could arrange.
(ii) The price that each senior citizen should be charged (to the nearest 10p).
b Find the best (cheapest) combination if there had been 220 senior citizens.

2 A travel agent planned an independent tour which resulted in the following costs per person:

Airfare £260 less 9% commission
Accommodation £210 less 8% commission
Sightseeing £10 no commission payable

If the agent used these costs less commission and then added a 15% mark up to fix a price, calculate the charge to the client for this holiday (to nearest £5).

3 The scale used on a map of Europe was 1 : 1 000 000. How many km were represented by a line of length 1 cm?

4 a If £413 is 35% of an amount of money, find the full amount.
b If £87.50 represents the 17.5% VAT on sales, find the sales.

5 A tour operator arranged holiday insurance at the following rates:

Holidays up to 10 days – £33 premium per person
Holidays up to 17 days – £37 premium per person
Holidays up to 24 days – £42 premium per person
Each additional week or
or part thereof £12 premium per person
Double premium for clients aged 70 years or over.

Calculate the cost of insurance cover for:

a Husband and wife (aged 34 and 30 years) holidaying 20 May until 9 June
b Gentleman aged 72 years holidaying 28 June until 6 July
c Lady aged 64 years holidaying 3 Aug until 5 Sept.

6 Refer to Meon Villa Holidays (page 54). John and Tricia Jacobs and their four friends wished to rent a villa for 2 weeks commencing 6 October. They would not pay more than £150 per person and they required a private pool. List the suitable accommodation (ignore travel costs which Meon would arrange).

7 On 4 February it is 22.55 in the UK: State the time and date in:

   a Canada (Pacific)   **b** Moscow.

8 A bank offers to buy yen at 250 to the £ and sell Yen at 234 to the £.

   a How many £s would you receive for 10 000 Yen?
   b How many Yen would you receive for £500?

9 A tourist drove out of Calais at 9.30 a.m. After travelling non-stop he passed a signpost at 1 p.m. showing the distance to Calais as 245 km. Calculate the tourist's average mph.

10 A travel consultant was paid £1925 commission on selling £5500 worth of insurance. Find the percentage rate on commission earned.

Test 8

1 A leisure centre charges £50 per annum membership fee and 80p per session for members. The session charge for non-members is £2.00. How much cheaper is it per year to pay the membership fee for a person who attends 2 sessions per week for 50 weeks of the year?

2 (Refer to the information provided on page 61 to answer this question.) A travel agent arranges for the Roberts family to hire a Sunny 1.3 for the period 3 October to 23 October whilst they were holidaying in Greece.

   a Calculate the cost of the car hire to the Roberts.
   b Find the commission received by the agency if the rate agreed with the hire company was 5%.
   c Calculate the total paid to the agency (to the nearest penny) if the rate of VAT on commission was 17.5%.
   d If the agency had an agreement with the car hire company to deduct the total due to the agency (commission and VAT) from the payment made by the client, find the amount sent to the car hire company.

3 The conditions relating to the cancellation of a skiing holiday were as follows:

Notification period before departure	*Amount to pay as % of holiday cost*
More than 42 days	Deposit
29–42 days	30%
15–28 days	45%
1–14 days	60%
Departure date or after	100%

A couple booked a skiing holiday costing £475 each to commence on 5 February. Between them they paid £150 as deposit.

a Calculate how much money would be lost by the couple if they had to cancel their holiday on 3 January.

b If they had taken out a cancellation insurance costing £18 each and they had reasonable grounds for cancelling their holiday, what would have been the total cost of their cancelled holiday.

4 A caravanner arrived at a camp site in the Lake District and took advantage of the mains electricity 'hook-up' system. He found that the maximum loading he could use was 5 amps.

a Would he be able to use an electric kettle which was rated at 900 watts?

$$\left(\text{Use the formula,} \ \frac{\text{Watts}}{\text{Volts}} = \text{Amps} \right)$$

b What *total* amperage would be required if the caravanner also wished to use a refrigerator rated at 100 watts.

5 A travel operator chartered a 120 seater aircraft to Madrid for £13 000 per return journey on 15 consecutive Wednesdays. If the operator assumes a load factor of 75% calculate the cost per passenger return trip (to the nearest £).

6 **a** Draw a pie chart that will show the following information:

Profit – £18 000, Labour costs – £36 000,
Overheads – £36 000, Direct holiday costs – £90 000.

b How many degrees represent the labour cost?

7 A coach hire firm quoted £10.50 per person to take 40 members of the British Legion the 166 miles from Leicester to Southsea to visit the 'Royal Marines Museum' and the 'D-Day Museum and Overlord Embroidery'.

Calculate the profit made by the coach firm given the following costs:

Labour (including the driver and administration) – £55
Fuel cost per gallon (bus average 8 mpg) – £2.30
Estimated Overheads – £32.00

Admission charges
Royal Marines – £2 per adult (10% discount for groups of 10 or more)
D-Day Museum and Overlord Embroidery – £3 per adult (50% discount for groups of more than 20).

8 An aircraft was due to depart Barbados 19.15 on 3 January. If the flying time is 8 hours 10 minutes, give the expected time of arrival at Gatwick.

9   A travel agent persuaded a couple to take a 3 week cruise from Southampton to celebrate their Golden Wedding. The cost of the cruise was £2075 per person. Return rail fare to the port was £56 each. If the agent received 10% commission from the Shipping Line and 7.5% commission from British Rail, find the total commission the agent earned.

10 A tour operator costed a holiday at £462. If the operator worked on a profit of 12% on turnover, what price should be charged for this holiday?

Test 9

The timetable reproduced opposite is taken from the British Railways 'Intercity Guide to Services'.

1   What is the main London station for trains to Edinburgh?

2   A passenger needed to arrive in Durham by 11.00 hrs. Which train would you recommend from London?

3   A man travelling by rail from Peterborough needed to arrive in Middlesbrough by 15.30 hrs.

   a   Which train should he catch?
   b   Would he need to change trains on the way?
   c   What is the expected length of journey?
   d   Could the man obtain a snack or restaurant meal on the train?

4   A passenger wished to travel from Darlington to arrive no later than 7 p.m. in Inverness. The passenger could not leave Darlington before 9.30 a.m.

   a   Which train should the passenger use?
   b   Give full details of facilities available and any connections to be made.

5   A lady is due to attend a conference to be held at an Edinburgh hotel. The conference commences with a reception on Wednesday evening at 5 p.m. She wishes to arrive one hour before the reception and the taxi journey from the station to the hotel takes approximately 20 minutes. What is the time of the latest train from Kings Cross the lady could take?

6   A man must travel the 325 miles from Peterborough to Glasgow and he is weighing up the differences between, and advantages of, travelling by train or car. He reckons by car he can average 40 mph but he would need at least two hours in rest stops. Cost is no problem as his firm will pay all expenses.

Calculate the time difference (and state which is quicker) between using his car and using the first available train with restaurant facilities.

1 London – Northeast England – Scotland

Full service London – Doncaster – York, Table 2. Other services Doncaster – Newcastle, Table 14.

Mondays to Fridays	C	C	C	C	C◨R	C	C	C	C◨R	C	C
					✕	⊠	✕	✕	➳y	✕	✕
London Kings Cross	—	—	0600	0650	—	0730	0800	—	0900	0930	
London Euston	—	—	—	—	0725	—	—	0835	—	—	
Stevenage	—	—	0620	0710	—	0750	0820	—	—	0950	
Peterborough	—	—	0657	0741	—	0821	0851	—	0947	1021	
Doncaster	—	0618	0805	—	—	—	0944	—	—	1118	
York	—	0727	0828	0852	—	0932	1007	—	1058	1142	
Northallerton	—	—	—	—	—	—	—	—	—	—	
Darlington	—	0756	0859	0923	—	1003	1038	—	1128	1212	
Middlesbrough	—	—	0949	1009	—	—	1113	—	1209	1246	
Durham	—	0815	0918	0942	—	1022	—	—	1157	1231	
Newcastle	0635	0830	0933	0959	—	1042	1108	—	1159	1251	
Sunderland	—	0910	1010	1040	—	1119	1149	—	1240	1319	
Berwick	0730	0921	1024	—	—	—	1159	—	1250	—	
Dunbar	0754	0945	—	—	—	—	—	—	1313	—	
Edinburgh arrive	0826	1016	1116	—	—	—	1250	1454	1345	—	
Edinburgh depart	—	1020	—	—	—	—	—	1510	—	—	
Glasgow Queen Street	—	1120	1220	—	—	—	1350	—	1450	—	
Glasgow Central	0925	—	—	—	1252	—	—	—	—	—	
Dundee	0955	1132	1346	—	—	—	1446	—	1546	—	
Aberdeen	1117	1248	1501d	—	—	—	1608d	—	1708d	—	
Stirling	0935	1135	1235	—	—	—	1405	1600	1505	—	
Perth	1022h	1222h	1255	—	—	—	1426	1638	—	—	
Inverness	1325g	—	1515	—	—	—	1720g	1920	—	—	

Mondays to Fridays	C	C◨R	C	C	C◨R	C	C	C	C	C
	✕	✕	✕	✕	✕		✕	✕	✕	✕
London Kings Cross	1000	—	1030	1100	—	1130	1200	1230	1300	—
London Euston	—	1025	—	—	1125	—	—	—	—	1325
Stevenage	—	—	—	—	—	1130	—	1206	—	—
Peterborough	—	—	—	1147	—	1217	—	1317	1347	—
Doncaster	—	—	—	—	—	1309	—	1414	—	—
York	1151	—	1221	1258	—	1333	1351	1437	1458	—
Northallerton	—	—	—	—	—	—	1430	—	—	—
Darlington	1222	—	—	—	—	1403	1442	1508	—	—
Middlesbrough	1308	—	—	—	—	1506	—	1538	—	—
Durham	1301	—	—	—	—	1422	1501	1527	—	—
Newcastle	1253	—	1316	1352	—	1437	1446	1547	1552	—
Sunderland	1340	—	1349	1419	—	1510	1519	—	1619	—
Berwick	—	—	—	1443	—	—	—	—	1643	—
Dunbar	1405	—	—	—	—	—	1557	—	1706	—
Edinburgh arrive	1432	—	1455	1534	—	1616	1628	—	1738	—
Edinburgh depart	—	—	1500	—	—	1630	1637	—	—	—
Glasgow Queen Street	1550	—	1620	1650	—	1720	1750	—	1850	—
Glasgow Central	—	1508	—	—	1654	—	—	—	—	1854
Dundee	—	—	1610	1748	—	1754	1816	—	1945	—
Aberdeen	—	—	1730	—	—	1920	1935	—	—	—
Stirling	1535	—	1600	1635	—	1719	—	—	1835	—
Perth	—	—	1619	—	—	1756	—	—	1927h	—
Inverness	—	—	1839	—	—	2005	—	—	—	—

Notes for this and opposite page:
A   Mondays to Thursdays.
B   Thursdays and Fridays only.
C   Fridays only.
d   Change Edinburgh and Dundee.
g   Change Edinburgh and Perth.
h   Change Edinburgh and Stirling.
s   Calls to set down only.
u   Calls to take up only.
x   Motorail London to Aberdeen.
y   Motorail London to Edinburgh.
z   Motorail London to Inverness.

Light printed timings indicate connecting service.

On-Board Services (see page 1):
ℂ   InterCity train with catering.
◨   InterCity Pullman train.
✕   Restaurant.
⊠   Restaurant (1st Class only).
Ⓢ   Silver Standard.
⊨   Sleepers.
Ⓛ   Lounge (1st Class only).
➳   Motorail service available.
ℝ   Seat reservations essential (free of charge).

7   A lady travelling from Newcastle needs to arrive in Perth sometime before 8 p.m. but does not want the bother of changing trains. Which train should she use?

8   A lecturer hoped to finish his speech in York in time to catch the 12.58 to Berwick. If he missed that train what is the earliest time he could arrive in Berwick?

Test 10

1 A caravanner wished to use the French auto-routes to travel to and from the South of France. He was informed that the charge for a solo car to travel from Calais to the South of France was 280 Francs. If the rate for the car and caravan was one and a half times the rate for the solo car, calculate the cost in £s sterling of towing a caravan on this holiday (to the nearest £).

2 A travel agent was requested to arrange a week's cruise on the canals of Burgundy (Bourgogne, France). A two-berth boat could be hired for 5060 Francs per week during the high season (4 July–28 August). Conditions for deposits were as follows: 25% of total cost on reservation, plus a further 25% at 3 months before embarkation, plus the final 50% at 3 weeks prior to embarkation.

    a Calculate the deposit required in £s sterling at the time of reservation if £1 = 9.85 francs (to the nearest £).
    b If the agency negotiated a commission of 12% with the French hiring company – what was the *total* earned? (To the nearest £.)

3 Find the time in Cardiff on 29 March when the time on the Pacific Coast of Canada was 02.30.

4 A travel agency earned £3010 through selling holiday insurance. If the rate of commission was 35% calculate the total value of insurance sold.

5 A caravan site opened on Saturday 19 May and closed on Sunday 21 October. The receipts for that period were £11 232.

Find

    a the average daily takings.
    b the number of visitors, if the pitch price was £6 and the average caravan contained 3 persons.

6 A travel shop offered to buy Japanese Yen at 268 to the £ and sell at 250 to the £. A returning tourist wished to exchange 75 000 Yen. How many £s sterling would she receive?

7 An hotel offered weekend breaks (Friday and Saturday nights) at a 35% discount on usual prices. The accommodation comprised of 35 double bedrooms and the normal charge was £52 per person per night.

Find the percentage occupancy over a weekend in October when the takings on accommodation amounted to £3785.60.

8 A potential tourist was told that the average rainfall in Florence during August was 38 millimetres. The tourist wanted this information in inches. What rainfall should be quoted if one inch = 25 mm?

9 Mr & Mrs Simpson are interested in spending 10 nights in Antigua (page 56). They would require half board terms. The travel agent suggests the Lord Nelson Hotel.

Calculate the total price quoted by the agent if Mr & Mrs Simpson wish to arrive in Antigua on 20 January after travelling British Airways Club World.

10 A motorist intended driving from Bristol to Edinburgh – a distance of 396 miles. He departed Bristol at 10.40 a.m., took one and a half hours over lunch and arrived York at 5.25 p.m. The car speedo showed he had covered 207 miles of his journey. The next day he spent the morning visiting York Minster and set off for Edinburgh at 1.25 p.m. The motorist stopped for a half hour tea break and arrived Edinburgh at 6.25 p.m. Give the average mph (driving time):

a From Bristol to York
b From York to Edinburgh
c For the whole journey

Test 11

1 Using the information given in Chapter 7, calculate the time a coach driver must cease driving on a day he starts at 8.30 a.m., takes the shortest possible break and drives the longest possible time.

2 The bursar of a college hall of residence hoped to recover all expenses during a year of 52 weeks. The normal college year was of 30 weeks duration. Income from students amounted to £3500 per week during term time. Expenses were as follows:

> Food and beverages – £1400 per week during term time.
> Labour and overheads – £1345 per week for the
> full 52 weeks.

There was a chance of three conferences on Tourism of equal length being held at the hall during vacations accommodating 30, 45 and 40 delegates respectively. The costs of food and beverages for these conferences would be £30 per head.

a Calculate to the nearest £1 the quote per person that the bursar should give to the conference organiser in order to cover all expenses for the year.
b The conference organiser replies that she will only take the hall at £75 per delegate. Should the bursar accept this offer if there is no possibility of other bookings? Give figures to support your answer (for discussion).
c If the bursar accepted the terms, calculate the expected costs to be covered for the year as a percentage of the total costs.

3   A tour operator was planning his Spanish holiday brochure
    using the following information:

    Accommodation costs per person per week – 40 500 pesetas
    less 8% commission
    Transfer costs per week – 9000 pesetas
    Aircraft Charter Costs (120 seater) – £18 000 per return trip
    for 15 consecutive Sundays.

    If the Operator assumes a load factor of 75%, calculate the price
    at which the holiday should be advertised if a mark up of 20% on
    costs is required. Use an exchange rate of 180 pts = £1. (Answer
    to the nearest £.)

4   When a British car is sold to a Belgian it brings money into the
    UK and is said to be an 'export'. When a Belgian tourist visits the
    UK and pays for 2 weeks at a British hotel does he act as an
    'import' or an 'export'?

5   A British Airways jet departs Heathrow 14.00 on 30 March and
    arrives Bangkok 07.55 the next day. Find the actual flying time.

6   (Refer to the information provided on page 61 to answer this
    question.) Chris intended to spend 7 days in Holland during July
    and he asked a travel agent to find the difference in cost between
    renting a Group A car on the continent and taking his own car.

    The agent found the single ferry fare for a car to Zeebrugge was
    £95 and the single car rate was £16 but the single foot passenger
    rate was £22. The Green Card insurance charge for Chris's car
    would be £10 per week but the car hire rate was inclusive of all
    insurance and damage claims.

    Find the difference as calculated by the travel agent and state the
    benefits of hiring a car (for discussion).

7   The Falcon Hotel has 75 double rooms and 50 single rooms. The
    nightly charge for a double room is £75 and the charge for a
    single room is £45. The guests tabular ledger showed the
    following rooms fully occupied.

	Mon	Tue	Wed	Thur	Fri	Sat	Sun
Double Rooms	40	40	30	35	50	60	45
Single Rooms	30	40	50	50	50	25	25

Calculate:
a (i) The total receipts from rooms for the week.
   (ii) The actual guest occupancy as a percentage of the
        possible guest occupance.
b Show the answer to a(ii) by means of a graph.

8   The food cost of a meal to a restaurant is £8.00. A gross profit of
    60% on the selling price is required and VAT is then added at
    the rate of 17.5%.

a What is the price of the meal to the customer?
b How much money is retained by the hotel (before food costs are deducted)?
c How much gross profit is made?

9 A motor insurance gives 17 days overseas cover free (green card). The charge for the next 10 days is £12. For each additional week, or part thereof, the charge is £7.

Calculate the cost of insuring a car for a driving holiday commencing on the 28 May and ending on the 5 July.

10 A tour operator's costs for a package holiday were as follows:

Accommodation – £235, Travel – £140, Administration – £10.

The operator worked on a profit of 30% on sales to price the holiday and then allowed travel agencies 10% commission on all sales.

Calculate the final profit earned by the travel operator on one holiday sold by a travel agent.

Test 12

The information reproduced below is taken from the 'Ski Yugotours' winter brochure and refers to the Yugoslavian resort of Bovec

Insurance rates per person: 8 days – £15, 15 days – £17

HOLIDAY PRICES

HOLIDAY PRICES PER PERSON IN £'s INCLUDING AIRPORT CHARGES

HOTEL	KANIN				ALP			
HOLIDAY NO.	9051				9052			
NO. OF NIGHTS	7	10	11	14	7	10	11	14
19 Dec – 27 Dec	246	309	323	372	239	299	312	358
28 Dec – 03 Jan	266	291	252	342	259	281	241	328
04 Jan – 10 Jan	189	222	242	265	182	212	231	251
11 Jan – 17 Jan	190	224	236	271	183	214	225	257
18 Jan – 24 Jan	199	233	246	279	192	223	235	265
25 Jan – 31 Jan	213	249	262	297	206	239	251	283
01 Feb – 07 Feb	226	264	277	314	219	254	266	300
08 Feb – 14 Feb	245	283	301	334	238	273	289	320
15 Feb – 21 Feb	263	292	301	334	256	282	289	320
22 Feb – 28 Feb	239	277	290	320	232	267	279	306
01 Mar – 07 Mar	227	262	275	305	220	252	264	291
08 Mar – 14 Mar	214	247	260	292	207	237	249	278
15 Mar – 21 Mar	201	236	248	281	194	226	237	267
22 Mar – 28 Mar	216	253	265	301	209	243	254	287
29 Mar – 04 Apr	229	253	–	–	222	243	–	–

	†HALF BOARD	†HALF BOARD
PRICES INCLUDE	Double: SH, WC	Twin: B/SH, WC
SUPPLEMENT PER PERSON PER NIGHT	Single Room £2.30	Single Room £2.30
3RD ADULT REDUCTION IN TWIN ROOM PER NIGHT	£2.50	£2.40
COT PRICE PER NIGHT	£2.25	£2.25

FLIGHTS

FLIGHTS to LJUBLJANA

GATWICK
(Sat, Sun, Wed)

HEATHROW
(Sat, Sun)

BIRMINGHAM
(Sun)

MANCHESTER
(Sun)

GLASGOW
(Sat)

Transfer time to resort
2½ hours – 87 miles (141km)

Note: Transfers usually via Italy.
Non UK passport holders usually require visa.

For flight details see page 41

IMPORTANT: see pages 38-40 for general information & Fair Trading Guarantee.

Remember to add: any flight supplements and insurance premium.

SKI PACKS

	6 DAYS		13 DAYS	
	Adult	Child under 11	Adult	Child under 11
BOOT HIRE Adult – size 35 + Child – size 35 –	£ 9.00	£ 6.75	£18.00	£13.50
SKI HIRE Adult – 140 cm + Child – 140 cm –	£18.00	£13.50	£36.00	£27.00
SKI SCHOOL	£22.00 (5x2 hours)	£22.00	£44.00 (10x2 hours)	£44.00
LIFT PASS	£30.00	£30.00	£60.00	£60.00

● Advisable for all skiers, photograph not required
● Valid for all lift numbers on the map

Extra day available and payable in resort only

Cross country equipment available and payable in resort only

Bookable through Yugotours Representative in RESORT ONLY

FREE SKI SCHOOL FOR YUGOTOUR GUESTS STAYING AT KANIN & ALP

GATWICK AIRPORT

DESTINATION	FLIGHT CODE	NO. OF NIGHTS	DAY OF DEPARTURE	DEPARTURES			APPROX. TAKE-OFF TIME	APPROX. HOME LAND	FLIGHT TIME	FLIGHT SUPPL.
NIS	NG61	7/14	SAT	22 DEC	-	23 MAR	13.55	13.00	2.40 hrs	NIL
LJUBLJANA	LG61	7/14	SAT	22 DEC	-	23 MAR	11.00	10.00	2.00 hrs	NIL
LJUBLJANA	LG71	7/14	SUN	23 DEC	-	24 MAR	13.30	12.30	2.00 hrs	NIL
LJUBLJANA	LG73	10	SUN	23 DEC	-	24 MAR	17.00	11.40 Wed	2.00 hrs	NIL
LJUBLJANA	LG33	11	WED	19 DEC	-	27 MAR	12.35	16.00 Sun	2.00 hrs	NIL

HEATHROW AIRPORT

BELGRADE	BH71	7/14	SUN	23 DEC	-	31 MAR	15.30	14.30	2.40 hrs	NIL
BELGRADE	BH73	10+	SUN	23 DEC	-	31 MAR	15.30	12.35 Wed	2.40 hrs	NIL
BELGRADE	BH33	11+	WED	19 DEC	-	27 MAR	13.20	14.30 Sun	3.20 hrs	NIL
LJUBLJANA	LH61	7/14	SAT	22 DEC	-	30 MAR	13.20	12.20	2.00 hrs	£5
LJUBLJANA	LH71	7/14	SUN	23 DEC	-	01 APR	13.20	12.20	2.00 hrs	£5

+10 nights holiday, flight inbound via Zagreb to London.
+11 nights holiday, flight outbound via Zagreb to Belgrade.

MANCHESTER AIRPORT

BELGRADE	BM61	7/14	SAT	22 DEC	-	23 MAR	13.50	13.05	3.30 hrs	£12
LJUBLJANA	LM71	7/14	SUN	23 DEC	-	24 MAR	13.15	12.30	2.30 hrs	£12

BIRMINGHAM AIRPORT

NIS (Via LJUBLJANA)	NB71	7/14	SUN	23 DEC	-	24 MAR	13.10	12.20	3.30 hrs	£8
LB71	LB71	7/14	SUN	23 DEC	-	24 MAR	13.10	12.20	2.20 hrs	£8

GLASGOW AIRPORT

NIS (Via LJUBLJANA)	NA61	7/14	SAT	22 DEC	-	23 MAR	13.15	12.30	4.00 hrs	£16
LA61	LA61	7/14	SAT	22 DEC	-	23 MAR	13.15	12.30	3.00 hrs	£16

1 **a** Calculate the total cost of 2 persons flying from Manchester, sharing a twin room at the Hotel Kanin during the 10 days period commencing 8 February.
b What is the expected time of arrival at the Hotel Kanin?

2 Mr & Mrs Scott and their 2 children (aged 7 and 10) are booked for 14 nights in the Hotel Alp during the period commencing 10 March. They will fly from Glasgow. All the family will need to hire skis, obtain a lift pass for 13 days and take out insurance.

Find the total cost of the skiing holiday allowing 30% discount on the basic accommodation for children under 11 years of age.

3 John Hall wishes to try skiing in Yugoslavia and a travel agent suggests he travels to Bovec and takes single accommodation at the Alp Hotel. John agrees to this suggestion and requests a 7 night stay during the period 22 March–29 March. He will need to hire boots and skis, attend the ski school and obtain a lift pass. John lives in Coventry and wishes to fly from the nearest available airport.

What is the price John will pay to the agent for this holiday?

4 **a** At Bovec the length of the Piste is 14 km. Express this distance in miles.
b The height of the top station is 2200 metres. Gives this height in feet if 1 metre = 3.3 feet.

5 At what time will flight LH61 depart Ljubljana on 2 January?

6 Jenny and Pete James arrange a skiing holiday including 7 nights at the Kanin Hotel. They will depart Heathrow on 23 December. They need to hire skis and obtain lift passes.

Find **a** the cost of their holiday
b their departure time from Heathrow.

7 Jeff, Richard and Michael book 11 nights in a twin room in the Hotel Alp commencing 20 January. If they fly from Manchester calculate the charge made by their travel agent.

Answers

1 Addition (page 1)

1	719	**2**	3009	**3**	1211	**4**	8166
5	10 641	**6**	4857	**7**	14 180	**8**	9168
9	10 hrs 12 mins	**10**	18 hrs 44 mins	**11**	19 hrs	**12**	32 hrs 25 mins
13	1.805 m	**14**	51.640 kg	**15**	4.425 m	**16**	8.255 litres
17	45.92	**18**	208.36	**19**	432.944	**20**	693.32
21	£86.85	**22**	362.10 Francs	**23**	206.22	**24**	£2.14
25	21.973 kg	**26**	182.58 kg	**27**	230.872 litres	**28**	43.134
29	23.79	**30**	105.935	**31**	465.442	**32**	£16.98
33	£602.13	**34**	£546.35	**35**	£414.94	**36**	£450.42
37	23.380 m	**38**	288.98 kg				

2 Subtraction (page 3)

1	403	**2**	1107	**3**	908	**4**	403
5	£28.55	**6**	£6.89	**7**	£172.82	**8**	£1564.82
9	8.62 F	**10**	$4.58	**11**	£76.51	**12**	£385.88
13	8.822 kg	**14**	3.925 kg	**15**	10.905 litres	**16**	1.75 m
17	8 hrs 5 mins	**18**	10 hrs 35 mins	**19**	8 hrs 38 mins	**20**	13 hrs 30 mins
21	3925 g	**22**	10 905 ml	**23**	1750	**24**	£20.89
25	£5.80	**26**	£1.69	**27**	£93.65	**28**	9.995 m
29	94.875 kg	**30**	£65.38	**31**	£37.91	**32**	1.743 kg
33	3.995 m						

3 Multiplication (page 4)

1	30	**2**	28	**3**	36	**4**	54
5	49	**6**	24	**7**	48	**8**	121
9	42	**10**	81	**11**	20	**12**	18
13	144	**14**	72	**15**	56	**16**	132
17	620	**18**	2961	**19**	718	**20**	5325
21	22 491	**22**	103 443	**23**	110.4	**24**	116.55
25	9.52	**26**	£74.16	**27**	£73.68	**28**	£5
29	£1082.16	**30**	£939.38	**31**	£991.32	**32**	£213.10
33	£660	**34**	£255	**35**	13.136 kg	**36**	12.240 litres
37	99 m	**38**	$15.81	**39**	163.20 Francs	**40**	DM71.5
41	£40.68	**42**	£20.16	**43**	£16.575	**44**	£182.50
45	£10 642	**46**	£750	**47**	DM275	**48**	$1720
49	Yen 2555	**50**	4728.5 kg	**51**	426.5 litres	**52**	4258 m

4 Division (page 6)

1	3	**2**	9	**3**	8	**4**	7
5	8	**6**	12	**7**	12	**8**	7
9	5	**10**	9	**11**	12	**12**	4
13	11	**14**	6	**15**	6	**16**	12
17	123	**18**	153	**19**	465	**20**	29
21	38	**22**	345	**23**	4206	**24**	3325
25	256	**26**	65	**27**	122	**28**	56
29	203	**30**	402	**31**	506	**32**	1.23
33	1.203	**34**	6.8	**35**	2.7	**36**	38
37	1670	**38**	2.46	**39**	8.525	**40**	3.5375
41	22.68	**42**	3.921	**43**	2.11	**44**	18.3
45	£181.46	**46**	14.224	**47**	207 km	**48**	18 kg

49 2.428   **50** £4.1876   **51** £0.51629   **52** 6.5 kg
53 8.205 litres   **54** 0.45 m

5   Problems using the four rules (page 9)

1 4 × 48, £600   **2** a £737.00   b 956   **3** £91.70
4 £4332   **5** a £105.45   b £131.10   **6** 10
7 £8.40   **8** a 310   b £385   **9** 25.7
10 a £6.75   b £3.75   **11** a 7   b 9   c 12   **12** £48.14
13 £166.25   **14** Apartment £59 cheaper   **15** 15 kg

6   Miles and kilometres (page 11)

1 527 miles   **2** 350 km   **3** 742 km   **4** 758 miles
5 a 169 km   b 255 miles   **6** 419 km   **7** 580 km
8 535 km   **9** 794 miles   **10** a 620 miles   b 2
11 a £20 cheaper via Portsmouth   b Ease of travel in the UK and France, Speed (Motorways), Cost of Motorways in France, Cost of fares for organiser, Availability of suitable Channel crossing, Length of Channel crossing.

7   Speed, time and distance (page 13)

1 7 hours   **2** 5 hours   **3** 3 p.m.
4 5 p.m.   **5** 13 hrs 20 mins   **6** a 2 p.m.   b 7 p.m.
7 a 280 miles   b 451.6 km   **8** Yes

8   Maps and plans (page 15)

1 $3\frac{1}{2}$ miles   **2** 15 kms   **3** 12 cms   **4** 2 m
5 13.75 m   **6** 50 kms   **7** 100 m   **8** 9 km
9 3 cm   **10** 1 km
11 A (i) 75 m (ii) 56.25 m (iii) 4218.75 sq m   B (i) 25 m (ii) 12.5 m (iii) 312.5 sq m.

9   Cancelling (page 17)

1 $\frac{5}{6}$ **2** $\frac{8}{9}$ **3** $\frac{1}{2}$ **4** $\frac{3}{8}$
5 $\frac{2}{3}$ **6** $\frac{1}{8}$ **7** $\frac{2}{3}$ **8** $\frac{1}{3}$
9 $\frac{2}{7}$ **10** $\frac{1}{4}$ **11** $\frac{2}{5}$ **12** $\frac{1}{3}$
13 a $\frac{17}{85}$ b $\frac{1}{5}$, five   c You decide.

10   Mixed numbers and improper fractions (page 18)

1 $\frac{5}{4}$ **2** $\frac{9}{2}$ **3** $\frac{31}{6}$ **4** $\frac{27}{8}$
5 $\frac{211}{100}$ **6** $\frac{23}{7}$ **7** $\frac{33}{3}$ **8** $\frac{51}{4}$
9 $\frac{126}{5}$ **10** $\frac{43}{20}$ **11** $2\frac{1}{2}$ **12** $4\frac{2}{3}$
13 $3\frac{3}{4}$ **14** $2\frac{5}{8}$ **15** $5\frac{5}{7}$ **16** $11\frac{1}{9}$
17 $4\frac{1}{7}$ **18** $6\frac{2}{3}$ **19** $5\frac{8}{11}$ **20** $3\frac{1}{2}$
21 $8\frac{1}{3}$ **22** $3\frac{1}{2}$

11   Multiplication of fractions (page 19)

1 $\frac{8}{15}$ **2** $\frac{15}{44}$ **3** $\frac{25}{48}$ **4** $\frac{6}{35}$
5 $\frac{2}{7}$ **6** $\frac{4}{11}$ **7** $\frac{1}{2}$ **8** $1\frac{1}{24}$
9 $1\frac{1}{15}$ **10** $3\frac{1}{8}$ **11** $2\frac{1}{2}$ **12** 15

13	$7\frac{1}{5}$	14	$13\frac{1}{3}$	15	$4\frac{1}{2}$	16	$5\frac{1}{4}$
17	$\frac{1}{6}$	18	$2\frac{1}{8}$	19	$\frac{1}{112}$	20	$\frac{1}{4}$

12 Percentages (page 20)

1	30%	2	25%	3	40%	4	2.5%
5	16.66%	6	52.5%	7	64%	8	17.5%
9	11.11%	10	80%	11	75%	12	81.81%
13	74%	14	4%	15	66.66%	16	2.5%
17	82.55%	18	50%	19	75%	20	20%

13 Percentage problems (page 21)

1 92% 2 Yes 3 6.66%
4 **a** 5.08% **b** £5.25 5 5% 6 **a** 7.5% **b** 6.25%
7 Self Catering 33.51%, Hotels 28.83%, Cruises 15.61%, Travel 22.03%
8 **a** 13.11% **b** 11.59% 9 35% 10 39.09%

14 Gross profit (page 23)

1 5% 2 60% 3 9%
4 **a** £24.20 **b** £19 loss 5 £78 6 20%
7 7.14% 8 63.10%

15 Net profit (page 25)

1 **a** £2750 **b** £810 **c** 8.1% 2 6.26%
3 **a** 5.53% loss **b** Lack of holiday sales in November
4 **a** £55 050 **b** £16 380 **c** 9.33% **d** 13.1%
5 8% 6 **a** 14.28% **b** 15.49%
7 **a** £11 990 loss **b** £11 990 **c** Advertising Town.
8 **a** 4.32% **b** 0.09% loss **c** Care must be taken over 'no surcharge' holidays.
9 £35 900

16 More about percentages (page 28)

1	£2.50	2	£58.95	3	$6.45	4	18.5 kg
5	£0.245	6	23	7	76	8	$4.50
9	£8	10	105 kg	11	£800	12	210 km
13	37.50	14	$160	15	£1.16	16	£9.75
17	£300	18	238 F	19	225 g	20	2700
21	£0.54	22	£10.08				

17 Commission (page 29)

1	£5040	2	£112.50	3	£121	4	£74.20
5	£6500	6	£188.75	7	£2502	8	£7330.50
9	£116.20						

10 Tip is optional gift by customer, Commission is agreed payment by employer
11 £1500

18 Discount (page 30)

1	£3072	2	£304	3	£235	4	£1536
5	**a** £5312.50 **b** To sell dated models	6	£126	7	£25.50		
8	£770						

19 Currency conversion (page 32)

1	L.154 700	**2**	£256.41	**3**	£20.32	**4**	£97.32
5	61p	**6**	591 F	**7**	£44.71	**8**	£502.56
9	£185.66	**10**	a L.215 500 b £93.69 c £6.00			**11**	£4.91
12	£240.38	**13**	a 2460 Swiss Francs b £943.39				

20 Percentage puzzles (page 35)

1	£5	**2**	£5	**3**	12 F	**4**	5 kg
5	£20	**6**	£16	**7**	$18	**8**	182 kg
9	£300	**10**	200 litres	**11**	$90	**12**	£150
13	£80	**14**	37.5 litres	**15**	1240	**16**	£1.75

21 Setting a price (page 36)

1	£710	**2**	£1500	**3**	£500 000		
4	a £6.25 b £10.13						
5	£56	**6**	£231	**7**	£466	**8**	£106.25
9	a £746 b £1940	**10**	35p	**11**	A £300 B £294		
12	a £6670 b £870	**13**	a £1825 b £500				

22 Days inclusive (page 39)

1	17	**2**	22	**3**	17th May	**4**	a 8 b 7
5	12	**6**	98	**7**	£18 900	**8**	£290
9	£71.50						

23 Twenty-four hour clock (page 41)

1	07.00	**2**	21.00	**3**	12.45	**4**	04.25
5	15.25	**6**	12.00	**7**	23.55	**8**	01.00
9	4 a.m.	**10**	1.30 p.m.	**11**	5.50 p.m.	**12**	12.05 a.m.
13	6.27 p.m.	**14**	3.10 a.m.	**15**	9.10 p.m.	**16**	10.30 a.m.
17	18.45	**18**	9.15 p.m.				
19	a 4.40 p.m. b 7.35 p.m. c 2 hrs 55 mins						
20	43 mins	**21**	4 hrs 45 mins			**22**	15 hrs 10 mins

24 Time zones (page 43)

1	75°	**2**	180°	**3**	Halfway	**4**	05.30
5	23.00	**6**	West	**7**	East	**8**	Ahead
9	Behind	**10**	17.00	**11**	06.00	**12**	22.00
13	07.45	**14**	18.30			**15**	05.00 (Aug 19)
16	18.40 (Mar 26)	**17**	3 p.m.			**18**	2 hrs 10 mins
19	1 p.m.	**20**	14 hrs 55 mins			**21**	1 p.m.
22	23.00 Sunday 13 January					**23**	10 hrs 35 mins
24	11 p.m.	**25**	09.30			**26**	45 mins
27	09.55	**28**	Thursday	**29**	Monday 31 December 1990		

25 Reading a timetable and fare table (page 48)

1	£89	**2**	£276	**3**	£144	**4**	£476
5	£144	**6**	1 Jan–11 July, 2 Sept–31 Dec			**7**	£84
8	2	**9**	5 p.m.				
10	a 1300 b (i) D (ii) C c £59.50						
11	a 13.45 b 14.45						
12	a 0900 b 13.00 c £90						
13	a £56.50 b 07.00 c 7 hrs 30 mins d 32						

14 **a** 13.00, 11th August **b** £380 **c** 11.45
15 Saturday, Sunday
16 **a** Concorde **b** 3 hrs 55 mins **c** Heathrow
17 **a** BA342, Heathrow Terminal 1, 12.30 p.m. **b** 1 hr 50 mins
18 3 hrs 55 mins **19** One **20** 1 hr 48 mins
21 **a** Heathrow 09.25 **b** 2 hrs 20 mins
22 **a** 11 hrs 20 mins **b** No **c** Mon, Thurs, Sat

26 Booking a holiday (page 54)

1 £129.75 **2** **a** La Clairiere **b** £146 **c** £1681
3 £460 **4** Peymeinade – half month **5** £1003
6 £260 **7** Auriou **8** £1968 **9** £1982
10 **a** £2907 **b** £3549 **11** £3118

27 Deposits and cancellations (page 57)

1 £65 **2** £180 **3** £450 **4** £15
5 **a** Stephen £15 **b** Paul £300

28 VAT (page 58)

1 £141 **2** £11.55 **3** £5550
4 **a** £21 **b** £141.00 **c** So that agency will retain the full 10% commission
5 **a** £72 **b** £12.60

29 Hiring a car (page 60)

1 £572 **2** **a** £476 **b** (i) £23.80 (ii) £38.08
3 £448 **4** **a** C, £850 **b** E2
5 **a** £194.25 **b** £38.85 **c** £44.68

30 Chartering (page 62)

1 £146 **2** £168 **3** £164 **4** £14
5 £113

31 Graphs (page 63)

1 £30 000 **2** November **3** £35 000
4 **a** £3000 **b** £2500 **c** £500 **5** £500 loss
6 £500 **7** Week 8 **8** Week 6 **9** 40
10 30 **11** Sunday **12** Colour improvement

32 Pie chart (page 66)

1 Male 240, Female 480 **2** Draw
3 Places of interest 72°, Entertainment 54°, Tours 36°, Accommodation 36°,
   Directions 144°, Others 18°
4 Food £80 000, Overheads £45 000, Labour £35 000, Net Profit £20 000

33 Mixed tests (page 68)

Test 1 (page 68)

1 17 hrs 5 mins **2** £136.17 **3** £605.46
4 £225 **5** £1.62 **6** £73.25 **7** 26 miles
8 171 miles **9** **a** 26.4 lbs **b** 15 kg **10** 15%

Test 2 (page 68)

1 **a** 00.05 **b** 20.15 **c** 22.20 **d** 07.45
2 9600 F   3 33.75 km   4 2.745   5 21.5 gals
6 **a** £111.50 **b** £249.50   7 £32.75   8 4 p.m.
9 **a** Mondays **b** Saturday, Sunday, Wednesday **c** £5600
10 12.5%

Test 3 page 70)

1 £862.50   2 Departs 09.00, Arrives 14.45   3 300
4 198°   5 **a** $\frac{4}{9}$ **b** $\frac{20}{21}$ **c** $\frac{1}{16}$
6 Route A by one hour   7 £52.63
8 **a** £6375 **b** £398.44 **c** £382.50   9 **a** 10 m **b** 4 m **c** 1 cm
10 56

Test 4 (page 71)

1 **a** £4270 **b** £14.94   2 **a** 6.20 p.m. **b** 4
3 £2891   4 6%   5 3 hrs 40 mins   6 £310
7 £160   8 **a** 36 mph **b** 30 mpg   9 £2190
10 4785 feet

Test 5 (page 72)

1 **a** 12 sq m **b** £87   2 Lost, £24 3 £341   4 £86.80
5 5 p.m., 31st Dec   6 £68.08
7 **a** 4 hrs 10 mins **b** £1331   8 £16   9 82.05%
10 35

Test 6 (page 73)

1 Yes   2 44.8 mph   3 1048 km   4 £176.25
5 Draw graph   6 60%   7 23 hrs 45 mins
8 £89.30   9 £2320.25
10 **a** (i) 65% (ii) 60% (iii) 62.85% **b** 54.83%

Test 7 (page 75)

1 **a** (i) 3 × 56, 2 × 25 (ii) £9.30 **b** 4 × 56   2 £505   3 10 km
4 **a** £1180 **b** £500   5 **a** £84 **b** £66 **c** £66
6 V. Auriou, Figanieres, Peyrebelle   7 **a** 14.55, 4th Feb **b** 01.55, 5th Feb
8 **a** £40 **b** 117 000 Yen   9 43.4 mph   10 35%

Test 8 (page 76)

1 £70   2 **a** £651 **b** £32.55 **c** £38.24 **d** £612.76
3 **a** £285 **b** £36   4 **a** Yes **b** 4.16 amps   5 £155
6 **a** Chart **b** 72°   7 £105.55   8 07.25, 4th January
9 £423.40   10 £525

Test 9 (page 78)

1 Kings Cross   2 07.30 Kings Cross
3 **a** 12.17 **b** Yes **c** 2 hrs 49 mins **d** Snack
4 **a** 10.38 **b** Light meals, Restaurant, Change at Edinburgh and Perth
5 11.00   6 5 hrs 8$\frac{1}{2}$ mins quicker by train   7 14.46
8 16.43

Test 10 (page 80)

1	£85	**2**	a £128 b £62	**3**	11.30
4	£8600	**5**	a £72 b 5616	**6**	£279.85
7	80%	**8**	1.52 inches	**9**	£3860
10	a 39.4 mph b 42 mph c 40.6 mph				

Test 11 (page 81)

1 5.15 p.m.   **2** a £90   b Yes, loss is £1765 instead of £6940   c 98.47%
3 £506   **4** Export   **5** 11 hrs 55 mins
6 £1 cheaper with own car, discussion (Wear and tear, damage cover, mileage
       depreciation, modern car etc.)
7 a £34 650 b 62.14% c Graph   **8** a £23.50 b £20 c £12
9 £26   **10** £110

Test 12 (page 84)

1 a £590 b 19.15   **2** £1443.20   **3** £290.10
4 a 8.68 miles b 7260 feet   **5** 11.20
6 a £598 b 13.20   **7** £714.60